Navigating the Politics of UX

Strategies and Stories from 40 Years in the Trenches

Volume 1: People

Recruiting Allies

Dispelling Myths

Changing Culture

Selling UX

John Scott Bowie

Navigating the Politics of UX: Strategies and Stories from 40 Years in the Trenches Volume 1: People

Publisher: Colorado Design Labs LLC Loveland, CO 80538
Author: John Scott Bowie
Cover Art: Mahmud Didar
Interior Design: Vivien Reis

Library of Congress Control Number: 2021923988

ISBN: 979-8-9851752-1-9

ISBN: 979-8-9851752-0-2 (ebook)

Printed in the United States of America

DEDICATION

This book is dedicated to all the user experience designers, managers, and thought leaders with whom I've had the honor to work over the past forty years. From you I have learned everything I know.

Keep up your good and important work. And thank you for making life a little simpler, a little easier, and a little more delightful, for the rest of us.

Never stop asking "What's Next?"

ACKNOWLEDGMENTS

Thanks to the employees of HP, GE, UnitedHealth Group, Deloitte, Microsoft, and Edmentum without whom this book would not be possible.

And thanks to the Marotti Writer's Retreat in beautiful Estes Park, Colorado, where the concept of this book evolved into a manuscript.

CONTENTS

Prologue: The Mission of UX

The internal UX organization operates at the center of the corporation, interacting and networking with every other department. This central role requires UX designers and managers to navigate competing priorities and political challenges unlike those experienced by any other functional area. Your responsibilities extend beyond effective collaboration; your job is to *influence* and *inspire* your colleagues to deliver world-class products and services.

Navigating the Politics of UX is a compendium of the challenges and opportunities I've faced during my four decades as a UX practitioner and leader. Over the course of my career, I've been a one-person UX department and built UX teams from scratch. I've led small UX teams in privately held companies, and managed large geographically dispersed UX teams in giant multinational corporations. Through trial and error, I've discovered several strategies for recruiting allies to the UX cause and advancing the corporate culture upward through Nielsen Norman Group's six stages of UX maturity.

Compared to the experience of outside contractors and consultants, the politics of UX are very different when you work fulltime inside a corporation. UX insiders are in it for the long haul. They are not assigned to just one facet of one project for one release; they are responsible for the full spectrum of UX activities across multiple releases. They must cultivate long-term working relationships with their internal partners in product management, development, support, QA, documentation, professional services, sales, marketing, and executive leadership—and repair these relationships when they're broken. They stick around to deal with the aftermath of a project—whether it succeeds or fails—and must learn from it to inform the next one.

I am writing this series of books for you—the UX insider—to help you pilot your career through the political challenges and opportunities that you are likely facing now or will face sometime in the future. You can read it from cover-to-cover to prepare for events that eventually will come your way or use it as a reference when specific political circumstances arise.

Navigating the Politics of UX comprises nine parts organized into three volumes:

Volume 1: People

Part 1: Cultivating Relationships—strategies for cultivating and sustaining relationships with partners in other functional areas.

Part 2: Fostering a UX-Driven Corporate Culture—strategies for dispelling persistent myths that prevent companies from achieving the highest stage of UX maturity.

Part 3: Designing a Supportive UX Microculture—strategies for crafting an inspiring microculture in which your UX team can thrive and contribute their best work.

Part 4: Selling UX—strategies for making the business case for UX initiatives and leading a breakthrough project.

Volume 2: Operations

Part 5: ReOps—strategies for funding, conducting, collecting, and deploying research to drive product roadmaps and design decisions.

Part 6: DesignOps—strategies for navigating the unique operational challenges facing UX practitioners in the day-to-day performance of their jobs.

Volume 3: Career

Part 7: Beginnings—strategies for UX education and training, transitioning to UX from other roles, interviewing for jobs, and managing the first five years of your career.

Part 8: Advancement—strategies for advancing your UX career, including forward and lateral moves, burnout, and no-win situations when your best option is to leave your current job and move on.

Part 9: Leadership—strategies for pursing excellence, visioning, and reimagining the practice of user experience design.

But First…A Word about Products and Services

To avoid saying "products and services" in every sentence, I will refer to both terms as "products"—meaning the things your customer buys and uses. From my perspective, UX design, product design, and service design are really the same thing:

When we design the user experience for a product or service, we define the actions people must take and the information they must know to achieve a result. This result can be achieved either by purchasing a product or by employing a service. For example, if the result I want is clean clothes, I can achieve this by operating a washing machine *product* or by paying for a laundry *service*. Each alternative has its own set of actions I must take and information I must know to get my desired result of clean clothes.

When I teach UX design to product teams, I encourage them to abandon the preconception that they are creating a product or creating a service. It could be either; it could be both. Instead, I teach them to imagine different "ways" users could achieve their desired results and to analyze the actions users must perform and the information they must know for each "way." Only then can the product team decide which "way" delivers the best experience and fulfills the company's business objectives.

PART 1
CULTIVATING RELATIONSHIPS

Every success and every failure in your career will be determined by how well you cultivate relationships with other people. Political battles are won and lost based on your ability to read people, recruit allies, understand others' motivations, and empathize with your coworkers' drivers and stressors.

When recruiting allies to your cause, you need to ask: What is the advantage for the person you're selling the idea to? What's in it for him/her?

Not every person can be recruited. You will encounter self-interested bosses and colleagues with whom you may never find common purpose. But, more often than not, you can survive and outlast these people by embracing one simple, albeit somewhat counterintuitive, strategy:

> *Your success* depends on your ability to make *other people successful.*

Recruiting Allies to Your Cause

As a UX professional, you can be a voice in the wilderness or the conductor of a chorus singing the same user-centric song. By yourself, you have limited power to influence the direction of your company. Your passion for UX can actually reduce your influence and isolate you as an unrealistic idealist.

To institute real change, you must recruit allies in as many other functional areas as you can. You must understand how your partners are measured, the goals that drive them, and how you can help them succeed. You must recruit partners in departments that previously have had no working relationship with UX.

Do this, and when important decisions and opportunities arise, you'll have a stable of advocates stepping up to support you.

To get started with your recruitment program, you need to go on a listening tour.

The Listening Tour

You should always conduct a listening tour when starting a new job, but even if you've held your current job for a while, it's never too late to expand your sphere of influence.

Ask your boss or someone who's worked at your company for a long time for a list of key people in the following functional areas (note: the roles and titles in your organization may vary):

- **Development:** project managers, product owners, business analysts, scrum masters, development leads, architects, data science leads, managers, and directors.

- **Product Management**: product managers for each product line, managers, and directors.

- **Quality Assurance**: QA testers, managers, and directors.

- **Marketing**: Collateral creators, social media and blog managers, brand managers, website managers, and directors.

- **Support**: call center agents, knowledge base content developers, field support personnel, managers, directors, and VPs.

- **Documentation**: technical communicators/content creators, editors, online help authors, managers, directors, and VPs.

- **Training and Professional Services**: Customer trainers and consultants, course creators, and implementation specialists.

- **Sales**: Territory managers/VPs, account managers, inside sales personnel.

- **IT and Internal Business Process Leaders**: If you support internal applications or processes (e.g., HR, business intelligence, manufacturing, and finance applications), include managers and users of these applications and processes.

- **C-Suite**: Division leaders, Chief Information Officer, Chief Technology Officer, Chief Product Officer, Chief Marketing Officer, Chief Strategy Officer, Chief, Operating Officer, Chief People Officer, Chief Financial Officer, Chief Innovation Officer, President, Chief Executive Officer.

- **Customers/Users**: Work with product managers, sales, and professional services to come along on customer visits. Ask for a list of customers who would be willing to get on a call with you.

- **Business-Specific Roles**: for instance, Chief Academic (education companies) or Chief Medical Officer (healthcare companies).

Don't limit your listening tour to colleagues in your immediate product team; your goal is to expand your influence beyond those with whom you work on a daily basis. Your new contacts will welcome your genuine interest in their roles and appreciate the opportunity to give input.

Once you have your list of people to talk to, send them an email introducing yourself, and ask for a 30-minute meeting. Meet with them in-person if possible, but a Zoom call works fine if they are remote. Include a list of questions you want to ask in your introductory message. Keep your list of questions to five or less and let the conversation flow where it needs to go.

The theme of your conversation with each of these key players is the same: What are your biggest challenges and how can UX work more closely with you to solve them?

Depending on their role, you might ask:

- What are your biggest challenges? What keeps you up at night?

- How would improving the ease of use of our products make your job easier?

- How much contact do you have with customers and users? What are they telling you? If you don't have contact with customers, would you like to?

- What are your impressions of the UX team? Is there something we could be doing that we're not doing?

- Can I follow up with you after I think about the things we've talked about? Would you be willing to offer feedback or collaborate with me on initiatives?

Listen empathetically to their challenges and concerns. Ask them to describe specific examples of their issues. Take notes and record your conversations if you can.

After you've completed several interviews, patterns and commonalities will start to emerge. Identify the most pressing problems that are shared across multiple functional areas.

Then, most importantly, *take action.* Conduct more research, implement new processes, and prototype possible solutions. Follow up with your new contacts after a month or two, explain what you've learned, show them your early solution prototypes, and ask them to help you refine them.

Once your ideas begin to produce results, publicize them as broadly in your organization as you can. Get on the agenda for department meetings, post stories on your company blog, and write articles for your internal UX newsletter. And always—*always*—give credit to the people in your listening tour who instigated the ideas.

My Story: The Invention of MENTOR

Within the first week of starting a new job, I set up a listening tour. I asked my boss for a list of people whom I could contact and set up 30-minute meetings with each of them. I interviewed both employees and customers.

I learned a lot from each interview, but the most impactful insights came when I tagged along on a customer training session with one of our professional services consultants. The customer had received product training only one week earlier, but when she tried using the product in more sophisticated ways, she realized she had forgotten most of what she had learned.

The training specialist walked the customer through the steps of each task, pausing frequently to let her take notes on the cheat sheet she was creating. I recorded the session with the camera on my iPhone, making sure not to include any personal identifiable information.

The customer called our product the "clicky system" because it took so many clicks to get anything done. At the end of the training session, the customer confided in me:

User: It just seems like it's longer and more convoluted than it has to be. I just want to be able to choose an <object> and then do what I want to do with that <object> from there. You can edit it. You can delete it. You can manage it or whatever. That's just an idea.

Me: That's a very good idea. That's why I'm here.

User: It just seems like it's so complicated to get to whatever…. She just told us last week how to do this and when it came time a few days later to actually do it, it was like Pfttt! And that's why we're having this meeting to write some notes down.

She didn't know it, but this user had just handed me the kernel of an idea that would result in one of the biggest innovations our company had produced.

When I returned to the office, I got to work creating a prototype with my UX team. We moved quickly through several iterations and within a few weeks we had a compelling, simple, and frankly really cool prototype to show to the leadership team.

At the leadership team meeting, I played the video of the customer's experience and suggestions. Everyone in the room was embarrassed by how difficult it was to complete each "simple" task.

Next, I showed them our interactive prototype and explained how it streamlined the user experience and solved for the customer's big unmet needs. To dial up the Wow! factor, we included animations and other elegant visual enhancements that made the demonstration even more compelling.

When my pitch was over, the CEO exclaimed, "This could be a whole new product!" The VP of sales just sat at the back of the room and smiled.

I departed the meeting to let the executives discuss what they had seen. My boss told me later that my demo had "blown up" the rest of the meeting and thrown out the current plan for the fiscal year roadmap.

At first, we called the new product "The Thing." But not long after the executive meeting, the head of marketing met with me to collaborate on a brand name. They hired an outside firm to come up with proposals, and we eventually settled on the name "*MENTOR*" (not the real name) and gave the new product its own logo.

While most of the UX team continued to feed the Agile machine, two of our experience designers were liberated from their other responsibilities to iterate on the new *MENTOR* concept. A few months later, we were ready to begin development.

The new product was one of the most successful releases in our company's history. All this was made possible by simply observing a customer, feeling her pain, and *listening* to her ideas for how to make her experience better.

There are so many people inside and outside your company with great ideas just waiting to be discovered. You just need to get out there and listen to them.

Seek the Common Goal

Once you have recruited allies to your cause, you need to keep them engaged. Because each functional area is accountable for a different set of metrics, conflicts often arise.

When you find yourself in these contests, call a timeout in the discussion and remind everyone that you share a common goal, even if you disagree on how to achieve it.

Try using this logic:

- Can we agree that we want our customers to be successful when using our products?

- Can we then agree that our company cannot succeed unless our customers succeed, that if they fail, then we fail also?

- And how do customers define success?

- Customers succeed when they achieve the results we promised them with as little hassle as possible.

Customer success is the metric everyone shares. So, when you find yourself in a disagreement with others about a decision you need to make, bring the conversation back to that common goal. Guide everyone through an analysis of each proposal by measuring its impact on customer success:

- Clearly state the decision you're trying to make or problem you're trying to solve.

- Allow everyone to propose their solution and why it makes sense given their metrics (we'll cover each functional area's metrics later). Listen with empathy.

- Let everyone describe how each proposed solution negatively affects their metrics (e.g., misses a deadline, exceeds a budget, is not technically feasible, etc.).

- Together, predict how each solution negatively or positively affects *customer* success.

- Evaluate your options. Choose one that increases the odds of customer success while minimizing the negative impact on business metrics.

This approach works well when the product owner, product manager, developer, and UX designer are debating design options for the current sprint. Often the final solution is a hybrid of the original proposals. Focus on the common goal and don't concern yourself with which idea "wins." Remember your success depends on making other people successful.

If the team cannot agree on a design, let the user be the arbiter of the decision. Prototype the competing options and get them in front of customers for feedback.

My Story: The Four-Legged Stool

If you are the manager of a UX team, the most rewarding sight you will ever see is the "Four-Legged Stool"—comprising the product manager, product owner, lead developer and lead UX designer—all gathered around the UX designer's computer, collaborating on a design.

Figure 1. Collaboration and the Four-Legged Stool

Perhaps you have had a different experience: the more common "throw it over the wall" approach to product development. In this scenario, work is performed in functional silos without consultation or collaboration with other members of the product team. The result: dysfunction, frustration, and rework.

In the *Cultivating Relationships with…* sections that follow, I describe strategies for building the Four-Legged Stool. You do this by understanding how your partners in the product team are measured, engaging them in UX activities, and applying your expertise and emotional intelligence to help them succeed.

I've worked in both "walled" and "un-walled" cultures and "un-walled" is a lot more fun. Everyone must feel free to contribute to any aspect of product development regardless of their role. UX designers have "visions" for the user experience; visioning and road mapping must not be the exclusive domain of the product manager. Product owners and developers have great ideas for information architecture, navigation, and UI design; these insights should not be discounted just because they didn't come from the UX team.

Dissolve the activity boundaries that separate development, product management, and UX into competing silos. Memorialize this operating principle in a written working agreement. You will still have separate departments and unique areas of expertise, but when it comes to research, visioning, design, and development, the core product team makes all important decisions—*together.*

Cultivating Relationships with Product Managers

> Action Plan:
>
> - Ask to come along the next time your product manager schedules a customer visit.
>
> - Convert the product manager's wish list of features into an interactive "vision prototype."
>
> - Solicit product management input throughout the design and development cycle.

What Drives a Product Manager?

Product managers are driven by the desire to design and sell market-leading products. They are accountable for managing the product budget, ensuring the product is competitive, conducting market research, and creating the short- and long-term product roadmap.

They measure success by meeting or exceeding revenue targets, winning competitive shootouts, increasing their products' Net Promoter Score (NPS), and managing releases to deliver on time and on budget.

How Can UX Help Product Managers Succeed?

The dependency of product management drivers on UX excellence might seem obvious: the better the user experience, the more likely customers are to buy your products and develop loyalty to your brand. But in their quest to maintain competitive parity, product managers often prioritize features over experience, favoring the addition of a new feature over repairing the broken experience with an existing one.

To begin cultivating a closer relationship with your product manager, arrange to come along on customer site visits. Make the case that you need additional user data to inform the design of features in the next release. If your travel budget is tight, set up teleconferencing calls or find customers close to the office that don't require a plane ticket and an overnight stay.

Make sure you interview and observe real users and not just the customers with the checkbook. Record their interactions, frustrations, suggestions, and impressions.

After the visit, debrief with the product manager. Categorize your observations into three areas:

- Features customers found difficult to use.

- Features customers wanted but didn't know existed until you showed them.

- Features and enhancements that customers would like included in future releases.

Discuss which of these observed experiences are most in need of repair, and how fixing the problem would increase NPS scores. Offer to prototype a solution when you get back to the office and work with development to estimate the cost of the fix.

After observing the user experience firsthand, visualizing the new and improved product in a prototype, and evaluating the cost of the fix, product managers are likely to include some of your UX enhancements in the next round of release planning.

To retain product managers as allies, engage them throughout the release cycle. Solicit their feedback as you think through design problems. Show them the iterations you've tried and discarded. Complement them on their suggestions. If they suggest changes that you disagree with, don't argue the point immediately. Instead, analyze their idea, compare it to alternatives, and share your conclusions at the next meeting.

Speak the product manager's language. Draw a connection between increases in the net promoter score and recent UX initiatives. Use UX metrics to prove how your design concept is superior to the competition's design for the same feature. Discuss how you can use these metrics to market the product. If you've shown your prototype to sales team, describe (and record) how excited they are to sell the enhanced features.

If your product has recently lost to a competitor in a product shootout, analyze the criteria on which the products were judged. There's a good chance the user experience was a key factor in the loss. Discuss how the shootout could affect sales (i.e., ask, how many prospective customers will pick number 2 over number 1?). Propose a UX project to address competitive deficiencies and show them a prototype.

If your product competes in a commodity market where all competitors offer the same features (e.g., computers, appliances), stress how the user experience represents your last competitive advantage. Dell understood this in an old marketing campaign: "Don't worry about mega-this and giga-that. Just tell us what you want to do with your PC."

In addition to collaborating on user research and design work, UXers can help product managers succeed by:

- Providing research data in an easily searchable and browsable repository to inform and defend product roadmap prioritization.

- Creating "vision prototypes" (UX roadmaps) that convert a list of features on a PowerPoint slide into a compelling, interactive story.

- Using UX metrics to compare the user experience pre- and post-release, proving that UX initiatives are reducing complexity and shortening Time to Results (TTR).

Product managers wield a lot of power in your company, including the power to prioritize or deprioritize UX initiatives on the product roadmap. Don't let a week go by without checking in with them.

How Can Product Managers Help UX Succeed?

UX designers cannot succeed without an alliance with product management—period. If your product manager doesn't grok the value of UX, you will be nothing more than an order taker responsible for converting a list of features into screens and workflows. You won't be invited to attend on-site visits, and thus won't have the user context needed to solve design problems. You'll spend your life staring at a computer screen, cranking out mockups with no way to judge whether you're making your users' lives better or worse.

Product managers are the primary conduit for setting up your user research program. Ask them to inform you of upcoming on-site visits and to introduce you to salespeople whom you can contact to schedule your own visits. Enlist their help in setting up user research sessions at conference expos. Work with them to set up a customer advisory council that meets every month to provide feedback on design concepts.

With the product manager as your ally, UX initiatives are less likely to be "one and done." UX stories are often scaled back to reduce the development effort when the schedule gets tight. That's okay—products need to ship and UXers must be willing to compromise. But compromise does not mean abandoning the original design forever. Your product manager can ensure your optimal design receives a high priority for delivery in the next release.

My Story: An Alliance of Opposites

Nielsen Norman Group surveyed product managers and UX designers to reveal overlapping views on job responsibilities. (See "PM and UX Have Markedly Different Views of Their Job Responsibilities" by Kara Pernice and Raluca Budiu, May 2nd, 2001).

They found that UXers and product managers often disagreed on:

which role was most responsible for product discovery,

- deciding what to research and which features to prioritize and build,

- developing the product vision,

- and ensuring research informs the product roadmap.

Territorial disputes of this nature are counterproductive, so how can UXers and product managers align their views of each other's responsibilities? The answer: celebrate the diversity of perspectives and collaborate.

I once worked for a department in which user experience, product management, and development all reported to the same executive leader. While this was an incredible amount of responsibility for one executive, in many ways it broke down silos and promoted empathy and cooperation among these diverse teams.

One time, all managers in this combined organization took a series of personality tests (Myers-Briggs and the like) and convened in a team-building session to compare results. The facilitator of the meeting instructed everyone to line up against the conference room wall based on their scores, one extreme on one end and the opposite extreme on the other.

To our surprise, the director of product management and the director of UX (me) scored on the extreme opposite ends of the scale. Based on the apparent dissimilarity in our personality types, you might expect that the product management director and I were constantly at odds with one another. But the opposite was true. Our two teams collaborated on virtually all aspects of customer research, product discovery, ideation, requirements prioritization, road-mapping, and feature design. We respected each other's role, shared responsibility, and were friends and partners.

This exercise revealed that Product managers and UX designers share the same goals but see the world very differently. When a product manager and a UX designer visit a customer, we ask different questions, observe different behaviors, and construct different but complementary insights. This diversity of perspectives is invaluable.

Cultivating Relationships with Product Owners

> Action Plan:
>
> - Include the product owner in all user research activities.
>
> - Negotiate the sequencing of stories with the product owner, moving those requiring more research and iteration toward the back of the sprint roadmap.
>
> - Be prepared to compromise when the schedule gets tight: accept an improved but less-than-perfect designs for the promise of revisiting the feature in the next release.

What Drives a Product Owner?

Sometimes the product owner and product manager roles are combined into a single role. In this book, I will assume these roles are distinct, with the product manager assuming primary responsibility the product vision, market research, and roadmap, and the product owner assuming primary responsibility for translating the roadmap into a sprint backlog and keeping the Agile machine running smoothly.

Product owners write user stories, oversee development planning, and monitor development progress. They expect the UX team to provide a steady stream of designs for development to build. If UX is ever to blame for shutting down the machine (blocking development and reducing velocity), there will be hell to pay.

Product owners are experts in the operation of their products and can be blind to UX defects. Having mastered their product's complex workflows, they may not realize that less expert users will have a problem.

Because product owners are largely driven by executing sprint plans and maintaining the development schedule, they are often at odds with UX designers when more time is needed to solve hard design problems. Product owners see themselves as the primary advocates and defenders of the development team, and if you're not careful, your competing priorities can damage the relationship.

How Can UX Help Product Owners Succeed?

Product owners often see themselves as having the final word in product decisions. The term "owner" suggests a level of accountability for the product's success equal to that of the product manager (and in some companies, they're the same person). To enlist the product owner as an ally of UX, you must convince her that the quality of the user experience is just as important as the quality of code that development is producing.

You do this by including product owners in all research activities. When they see first-hand the impact of the user experience on the products they "own," they will defend UX initiatives with the same zeal as they do development requirements.

Nurturing the product owner's empathy for the user helps you negotiate more time to iterate on important features. During sprint planning and story prioritization, work with the product owner to schedule backend stories early in the cycle, and delay UX-intensive stories until later in the sprint roadmap.

Be honest with the PO when you need more time to solve a hard design problem. Show her a video clip from your user research to remind her how challenging the feature is:

"Remember how that customer in Dallas was so frustrated when she tried to use this feature? I need more time to get it right. Can we delay bringing this feature into sprint for two more weeks?"

Once you have recruited the product owner as an ally, the answer will almost always be yes.

Both product owners and UX designers benefit when UX work is out of phase with development work by several weeks or months. Because the UX designer is responsible for researching and iterating a design before development starts *and* shepherding the design through the sprint, this may seem impossible, but it's not.

Big Design Up Front has a negative connotation in the Agile community. Practitioners believe it is just waterfall by another name. While "Sprint Zero" supposedly provides sufficient time for design work before development sprints begin, it rarely accounts for the research, think time, and iteration required for complex new features, and it certainly doesn't accommodate the effort required for designing entirely new products. While Agile development purports to accommodate changing requirements and "Ah-ha!" design breakthroughs, in my experience it rarely does.

So, what's a UX manager to do? Three things:

- Make sure your designers know that compromises to the user experience may be required to meet the schedule (and keep the product owner happy). They must understand that as long as the experience is improved—even though it's not as good as the designer wants it to be—they should consider the release a success. However, the product owner (and product manager) must agree that design work that was sacrificed due to schedule constraints must be moved to the top of the backlog for the next release.

- I say again: invite the product owner to attend all research activities: on-site customer visits, Zoom calls, and usability tests. Make sure your research program is continuous, not just front-loaded at the beginning of a project. When product owners see users struggling to get results with the product they "own," they are more likely to balance their mandate to maintain development velocity with the time required to repair the current experience. Remind them of the Agile Manifesto principle that states, "Our highest priority is to satisfy the customer through…delivery of *valuable* software."

- Over time, progressively move UX work out of phase with development until design begins one to three months before coding starts. This gives you time for more research, more iterations, and more time for "Ah-ha!" discoveries. Invite development to collaborate with you in this early design phase, but make it clear that you're discovering and prototyping, *not* writing production code. If development insists on continuous production coding, carve out a couple of members of your UX team to work on the early experimental design phase while the rest of the team feeds the Agile machine.

I'll have much more on this strategy in Volume 2, *Part 5: DesignOps.*

How Can Product Owners Help UX Succeed?

As stated earlier, product owners can help UX succeed by prioritizing UX quality as highly as code quality. Just as some features take longer than expected to develop, UX design can take longer than expected to get right.

In the Agile development world, a "spike" is a story aimed at answering a question or gathering information instead of producing shippable code. Product owners need to understand that, in addition to technical spikes, UX spikes may be needed to solve a hard design problem (i.e., answer a question) or conduct more user research (i.e., gather information).

Convincing product owners of this may require a dramatic change to the product owner mindset. Rather than go in depth here, I'll provide several strategies for change minds and dispelling myths in the next section—*Cultivating Relationships with Developers*—and in *Part 2, Fostering a UX-Driven Corporate Culture.*

My Story: UX Is to Blame for Everything!

Shortly after accepting a job as the UX director at a new company, I had an injury that forced me to work from home for several weeks. About three weeks into the job, I had a meeting with the chief product owner and the director of development. They spent the entire call telling me how UX was to blame for dragging down sprint velocity and was constantly antagonizing the development team with insistence on pixel-perfect adherence to mockups. The schedule was slipping badly. They were concerned—and rightly so—that they would be held accountable to the leadership team if the release date was missed.

I had inherited this problem and, being new to the job, had not had time to fix it. Never mind that the UX team was badly under resourced; we had two designers to support three sprint teams, each working on a different product, all of which were releasing on the same date. But staffing up would take time, and we needed an immediate solution.

So, for the duration of the next release, the UX team devolved into a mockup factory. We turned out wireframes at an incredible pace with little consideration for the quality of the experience we were providing to our users. We conducted no research. We had no time for iterations. Our sole objective was to feed the Agile machine.

In a few weeks, the development schedule was back on track and Agile metrics were in the green again. UX-wise, the release was nothing to be proud of, but I had earned the trust of the product owner and the development director. Had I not achieved this objective, all future releases would have been at risk.

The relationship did heal, and over time we became great friends and colleagues. With each subsequent release, we moved UX work a little further ahead of development, affording us adequate time for research and iteration.

The moral to the story is this: you must achieve both design and political objectives, but sometimes you can only accomplish one objective at a time.

Cultivating Relationships with Developers

Action Plan:

- Sit down at a developer's workstation and offer to co-author the CSS with her.

- Develop as many as three solutions to a given design problem, ranging from the best UX and hardest to build to good UX but easiest to build. Be ready to compromise when the schedule gets tight and revisit the design in the next release.

- Become a UX engineer by convincing development that the user is a component in the system architecture and that the system must be designed to accommodate human constraints.

What Drives a Developer?

In the Agile world, developers are measured by lead and cycle time, throughput, work in progress, work item age, flow efficiency, and other Agile metrics. In other words, they are measured on how fast they can pull stories off the sprint board and by the speed at which they can correct bugs in their code.

Twenty-five years ago, before user experience design became a recognized profession, developers were responsible for both design and development. User research was nonexistent. The emphasis on working technology over working human beings had produced products that were challenging to use by all but the most determined technophiles. Alan Cooper wrote a passionate and entertaining book called *The Inmates are Running the Asylum* back in 2004 that documented the dominance of engineering culture.

Today, most developers rely upon UX designers to provide visual and interactive representations of features and workflows before they build them. Our design specs and mockups free them to focus on their passion for producing elegant, efficient code.

Developers are just as creative as UX designers. They find it rewarding to discover ingenious solutions to hard technical problems. One development manager I worked with put it this way:

"We want to design software, not crapware."

Making things work drives developers. What *drives them crazy* are continuous and unexpected changes to features they've already built. In theory, The Agile Manifesto…

…welcomes changing requirements, even late in development. Agile processes harness change for the customer's competitive advantage.

According to this principle, Agile developers should accommodate late-breaking UX discoveries if they improve the user experience. But in the real world, given all the Agile metrics developers are accountable for, rework is painful.

How Can UX Help Developers Succeed?

You have likely encountered a wide range of developer attitudes: some care deeply about user needs and have great insights for improving the UX design; others have zero empathy for users and just want to be left alone to write code. While user empathy in a developer is desired, it is not required to produce simple and usable products.

Rather than viewing design and development as separate responsibilities, UX designers and developers should collaborate on both. Developers should attend user research sessions and help solve design problems. UX designers should sit down at the developer's workstation and collaborate on coding the CSS. UX designers and developers should team up on a design system with attached code libraries to make both the design and development processes more efficient.

Communication and credit-sharing is essential. If a developer improves upon the UX designer's original mockup, the UX designer should acknowledge the developer's contribution during standup meetings and retrospectives. If the sprint schedule forces the premature delivery of mockups to development, the UX designer should warn the developer that changes are likely after more research and iterations are completed. UX designers should always be willing to adjust the "perfect" design if it is not technically feasible or will take too long to build. The "perfect" design can be revisited in the next release.

How Can Developers Help UX Succeed?

Developers transform UX designs from concept to reality. Unless they are willing to expend the effort required to implement the feature as designed, the UX designer's work—no matter how innovative—will never be shipped to a user.

One of the tenets of the original "HP Way" promoted by Bill Hewlett and Dave Packard was MBWA—Managing By Walking Around. Every employee was encouraged to regularly walk by their colleague's desk and ask, "How's it goin'? Anything I can do to help you? Any questions I can answer?"

Fostering this kind of collegial relationship with development partners helps the UX designer catch small—and sometimes large—deviations from the design while there is still time to correct them. During these informal check-ins, the developer and designer can discuss acceptable workarounds and discover improvements to the original design.

But the primary way developers can help UX is by being openminded to, and supportive of, the rationale for the experience design. This may require a radical change in mindset in some development organizations.

You must convince developers that a user's failure to easily achieve results with the product is also their failure.

The first step in this mind-shift is to invite developers to get out of the office and come along on customer visits and attend usability tests. They need to witness firsthand how the user-product interface determines whether their elegant code is used or not used.

Empathetic developers will be embarrassed by the user's struggles and immediately grok that the user experience needs to be fixed.

Non-empathetic developers will require more convincing. If the research reveals that users can't find or use a feature, you should commiserate with the developer. Tell him or her...

"It's a shame people aren't using that feature you spent so much time and effort developing. But I can help you with that. If we just tweak the user experience a little bit, users will easily discover the feature and will love using it. Let me put a concept together and get back with you."

Show the developer a prototype of your redesign, explain why it is simpler to use, and assure him or her that the new design retains all the feature's current capabilities.

Finally, you need to dispel the myth that you design, build, and sell *products* and that your products have *users*. These myths are discussed in detail in Part 2, *Myth #1* and *Myth #7*, but I'll provide a few thoughts here on how to change this mindset in developers.

You must express the user experience in engineering terms. Make the case this way:

Ask the development manager to invite you to speak at their next team meeting or offsite. Explain that you've finished conducting user research or usability testing and you'd like to discuss your findings.

Begin the presentation by showing videos of your research and summarizing your findings. Next, ask the group this rhetorical question:

By itself, without user interaction, what can our product accomplish?

The answer, of course, is nothing. Products require human beings to press buttons, click menus, turn knobs, and pull levers to achieve something useful. Services require users to navigate spaces, comply with policies, and follow procedures to achieve their desired result. So, for a product to function properly, its user must "function" properly.

The user gets all the functionality leftovers after the product is developed. It's as if we're saying to our user (use a real user's name if you can), "Here's what we'll do, and here's what you have to do to get the results you want. Take it or leave it."

Emphasize that every time you design a product, you automatically (and usually unconsciously) design its user. Your user design spec includes such things as terminology the user must know, concepts the user must understand, tasks the user must perform, virtual or real spaces the user must navigate, objects the user must find, error conditions the user must troubleshoot, and documentation the user must read.

Taken together, these requirements constitute the design of your ideal user—a human being who will serve as the perfect complement to your product. If you sell your product only to customers matching these design requirements, the user-product system will accomplish everything it was intended to.

Now the bad news: no such ideal "user" exists. Our only recourse is to design your products to accommodate the technical constraints of the human component in the system.

My Story: Empathy Desired but Not Required

I once worked with a lead software engineer who was just not wired for empathy.

We exposed him to users as much as we could, but he was unmoved. We invited him to design thinking workshops, but he always sat at the back of the room and participated as little as possible. All he wanted was for someone to hand him a set of requirements and send him back to his desk to write code.

Nevertheless, we still found a way to make him care deeply about UX.

Paradoxically, empathy for humans is not required to produce a human-centered design. Non-empathetic minds are often motivated to design reliable, working *systems*—a system that includes a functioning *human component*.

We convinced this developer to view the human component as he did the technology components: a device with I/O capabilities, encumbered by bandwidth and memory limitations, and prone to a host of random errors. Because user constraints are absolute, he must engineer the technology components to accommodate them.

We helped the developer recognize that the human component was the most susceptible to failure and thus most likely to bring the whole system down. He would never make function calls or data requests to a component that lacked the ability to execute them. Likewise, he can't design a successful system that expects the human component to do things it's not programmed to do or to supply data it does not have.

He eventually grokked that his elegant technology was useless unless the human component could successfully execute the functions that the system had assigned to it.

By accepting responsibility for the reliability of the entire system—including the human component—the engineer was able to appreciate the UX contribution to his work and build usable human-centered products, even without empathy for the user.

Cultivating Relationships with Support

Action Plan:

- At least once per month, spend a few hours listening in on support calls.

- Working with support, develop design solutions to the most common call center issues and measure the impact on call volume after deployment.

- Propose a joint project with the support team to reduce routine calls by embedding support assets into the product itself.

What Drives a Support Professional?

Most companies staff call centers, either to assist employees with internal applications or to answer customers' questions and help them resolve product issues.

Call center agents are amazing human beings. They keep their cool in the face of abusive behavior while diagnosing and treating whatever bad experience the customer is calling about. Even though they owe their jobs to users' inability or unwillingness to solve their own problems, exasperated agents often hang up the phone and exclaim: "Why don't these people just Read The F...riendly Manual!?" Hence the acronym RTFM that's been around for decades.

Support professionals don't spend years mastering complex technology just to become a manual reading service. They don't enjoy spending eight hours a day walking callers through the same how-to procedures over and over again. Yet, these scenarios comprise a large portion of their jobs.

The support organization may be the only department in the company whose charter is to reduce the need for itself. On low-margin products, one support call can wipe out all profit from a sale.

Support costs are often scrupulously measured and reported as:

- Calls per product sold

- Call duration, with specific targets

- First call resolution percentage, again with targets

- NTF (No Trouble Found) product return rates

While the support organization is accountable for these metrics, it has only limited ability to control them.

How Can UX Help Support Professionals Succeed?

No organization in the company feels the pain of a poor user experience more acutely than the support department. If you don't have a symbiotic relationship with support, including a closed feedback loop between support issues and user research findings, you're missing a huge opportunity.

Most of the metrics for which the support organization is accountable can only be controlled by improving the user experience. Therein lies the natural partnership between the two teams: rather than constantly reacting to user problems, support engineers would much rather work proactively with UX to solve them.

The call center data that the support team publishes every month is second only to field research in its utility for identifying and fixing user experience problems. The closed feedback loop between UX and support should work like this:

- Support reports the most frequent "How do I…?" calls to the UX team.

- The UX team, with the help of call center agents, design solutions to mitigate the reasons for the calls.

- The support team tracks the effectiveness of the mitigation by measuring the subsequent decline in call volume for the issues.

- UX and Support collaborate on a report that documents the repairs to the user experience and the resultant decline in support calls.

- The executive leadership team recognizes UX and Support for their collaboration and initiative.

How Can Support Professionals Help UX Succeed?

Support is a UX job. Like UX, support is responsible for helping users achieve promised results with the company's products, albeit via different means and channels.

To enlist support's help, you simply to engage them. Use support data to inform UX priorities. Work with support engineers on troublesome UX issues and include them in ideation and design thinking workshops. Afford them the respect they deserve as experts on the voice of the customer.

Every month, UX designers should spend half a day listening to incoming support calls. Take lots of notes; quoting customers' frustrations is valuable evidence for supporting UX initiatives.

After releasing a UX enhancement that addresses a common support issue, quantify the support cost savings in financial terms. You need only one cause-and-effect story showing the direct correlation between a UX redesign and a reduction is support calls to pave the way for future proposals.

My Story: The Evolution of Integrated Support

I've experienced both good and bad relationships with support.

Early in my career, I proposed a partnership with support to address usability problems. The support manager responded:

"We don't want to make our products *too* easy to use. We make a lot of money selling support contracts."

In his mind, complexity was a business strategy. I hope his attitude, and the goal of sustaining support contract sales, has gone the way of the dinosaurs.

Several years later, I joined a support team to design and deliver self-service support offerings via the Internet. We hoped a robust e-support program would reduce customers' reliance on the call center to answer their questions.

We rewrote our internal support documents using language appropriate for a consumer audience and published the information on our support website. While we made a dent in the call volume, we didn't solve the underlying problem. Support remained a separate channel that required users to abandon the product and redirect their attention to navigating the support site with no guarantee they would find the solution to their issue.

My UX/Support breakthrough came at another company. We realized the key to getting customers to use self-support was to embed our support offerings directly into the user experience of our products. Support was no longer a separate channel; information was delivered at the time and place it was needed.

We hired an omnichannel support expert and a UX writer to develop the strategy and author the content. We created product tours, step-by-step walkthroughs, 60-second videos, and pop-up lessons. Users could choose how they wanted to consume information, from "help me do it" to "show me how" to "tell me more."

Through this collaboration, the UX team became an extension of the support organization and support became an extension of UX. Another functional silo was shattered, and the customer and the company were better for it.

Cultivating Relationships with Quality Assurance

> Action Plan:
>
> - Form a working group with the QA team to classify and prioritize UX defects.
>
> - Meet weekly, daily, or as needed with QA and development to review and resolve UX defects.
>
> - Celebrate and publicize the increase in Net Promoter Scores resulting from finding and fixing UX defects before release.

What Drives a Quality Assurance (QA) Professional?

Quality Assurance professionals are responsible for ensuring the company's products are released with as few defects as possible. They develop tests—both manual and automated—to detect defects, classify them, and assign them to the responsible party to resolve.

In the Agile world, QA is not a separate phase toward the end of the release, but an integral part of development that occurs continuously throughout the product lifecycle. In the spirit of agility, QA professionals are driven to detect, assign, and clear product defects as early as possible.

QA testers are often measured by:

- Mean time to detect—the average time it takes for the QA team to detect a bug.
- Mean time to repair—the average time it takes to correct a problem.
- Rejected defects—percentage of defects that were rejected by the development team because they have already been reported, cannot be reproduced, or are incorrect.
- Escaped defects—problems that were not detected during the QA cycle but were reported after product release.

How Can UX Help Quality Assurance Professionals Succeed?

Invite the QA director to accompany you on user research visits, Zoom interviews, and usability tests to see firsthand all the "escaped defects" QA is missing—UX issues that are preventing customers from easily achieving promised results.

Express UX defects in QA terminology: functional defects are function calls to customers for which no functionality (knowledge) is preinstalled; performance defects are slowdowns in Time To Result (TTR) when customers are forced to call support or search documentation to get help.

(Note: the QA team may already classify some issues as "usability" defects, but extending functional and performance defects to include the "function" and "performance" of the user may elevate these defects in severity and priority.)

QA gets credit for finding bugs, but rarely are their activities correlated to financial performance. You can help with this: At least once a year, work with QA testers to identify their top ten found issues. Apply the business case criteria discussed in Part 4 to estimate the financial cost to the company had these issues *not* been found and corrected. Consider lost revenue from angry customer reviews and defections, support costs, R&D costs wasted on unused features, etc. Ask your CEO to report and celebrate the savings attributable to QA performance at the end-of-fiscal-year company meeting.

Further enhance the eminence of the QA/UX relationship by linking UX defects to Net Promoter Scores. If the bug count and the NPS score are both low, make the case that finding and fixing only technical defects is insufficient to move the NPS needle. There must be another type of "bug" that customers are noticing. Propose that QA and UX work together to track and fix user experience defects. When the NPS score begins to rise, draw the connection between identifying and correcting user experience defects and the improved customer perception of the company's products.

How Can Quality Assurance Professionals Help UX Succeed?

Advancing your company toward a UX-centered culture takes time, but collaborating with QA is a good place to start. Your challenge is to convince QA to record user experience problems as product defects and to classify and prioritize them appropriately.

In theory, all deviations from Agile Principles should be recorded as defects, especially these:

1. "Our highest priority is to satisfy the customer through early and continuous development of valuable software." Application to UX: *Software that impedes or prevents customers from achieving promised results is* not valuable.

7. "Working software is the primary measure of progress." Application to UX: *Software must do more than just "work;" customers must succeed at* making it work.

9. "Continuous attention to technical excellence and good design enhances agility." Application to UX: *Good design does not apply only to software architecture; it includes* good user experience design.

10. "Simplicity—the art of maximizing the amount of work not done—is essential." Application to UX: Simplicity—*the art of maximizing the amount of* work not done by the user—*is essential.*

Jeff Gothelf's and Josh Seiden's book, *Lean UX*, provides valuable advice for making UX work with Agile, but until UX principles are infused into the development culture, we must work with QA to log UX deviations from these Agile Principles as critical and serious bugs.

Lobby the QA director to launch a working group to diagnose and classify UX obstacles as product defects. Develop a heuristic checklist to aid in classification and regularly meet with QA testers to review UX defects and issue tickets.

Reach agreement that deviations from mockups should be considered violations of acceptance criteria. This doesn't mean development can't propose changes, only that changes cannot be implemented without sign-off from the Four-Legged Stool (UX lead, product owner, product manager, and development lead).

Finally, reach agreement that usability tests are part of the QA process and that any failures found therein should be logged as critical performance defects.

My Story: QA, Integrated Support, & Front-End Development

In the last section, *Cultivating Relationships with Support*, I described how we embedded support assets into the product UI. This also afforded us the opportunity to work more closely with QA.

Our integrated support deliverables were QA tested as thoroughly as any other software component, and the UX team was accountable for resolving all critical defects before the product could ship. Like the development and QA teams, our lead integrated UX designer was on call the night before a release to fix any last-minute surprises.

As the boundaries between user experience designers and front-end developers continue to dissolve, UX involvement with QA must strengthen as well. In several of my jobs, our senior UX designers were competent HTML, CSS, and JavaScript developers. On one occasion, a junior developer rejected a UX designer's mockup, justifying the denial by declaring the design was not technically feasible. The UX designer responded by delivering, not just the mockup, but the code to implement it as well.

At its core, UX is an engineering discipline. You are responsible for coding functionality that runs reliably on the human processor in the User-Product System. You are accountable for ensuring seamless interoperability between the human component and the technology components as they work together in the pursuit of results.

As the perception of your UX team evolves from artists to architects, leverage these opportunities to strengthen your relationship with QA. I'll go deep into UX Engineering in Volume 2 of this series. For now, understand that the UX/QA partnership will be instrumental to your success as you advance your corporate culture up the UX maturity scale.

Cultivating Relationships with Documentation

Action Plan:

- Ask a writer to review and improve the language elements in your designs.

- Collaborate with technical communicators on your design system to ensure language appropriateness and consistency.

- If your manual writers are resistant to transitioning to UX writing, send them to me. I will help them work themselves out of a job and into a better one.

What Drives a Documentation Professional?

I started my career as a technical writer. I was an English major in college and when I couldn't find a writing job after graduation, I went back to school to study a more marketable discipline: computer science.

After one semester of grad school, I got an internship at Hewlett-Packard (HP) in Fort Collins, Colorado as a programmer. My assignment was to design and code a desktop application to predict warranty costs for the computer workstation division.

I failed miserably.

A few weeks before the end of my internship, I saw an interesting opportunity posted on the internal job board, a job called "technical writer." I had never heard of this position before, but it seemed like the perfect job for me due to my training both in writing and computer science. I got the job and never returned to grad school.

What drove me is a technical writer? A love of language. A love of problem solving. A love of structuring information for clarity and findability. A love of translating the operation of complex technology into simple, concise procedures.

At the start of my tech writing career, I measured the quality of my manuals through the traditional metrics of clarity, conciseness, completeness, accuracy, and grammar. But I soon discovered that the ultimate measure of documentation was *effectiveness:* the percentage of users who actually *read* and *used* what I wrote. And if that percentage was low, how could I better employ my expertise to deliver true value to my customers?

How Can UX Help Documentation Professionals Succeed?

The technical communication profession has been reinventing itself for several decades. It has evolved from written manuals to online help systems to performance support systems to self-help websites and, most recently, to UX writing. This is a good thing.

Technical communication has become a sub-discipline within the UX profession in the same way that visual design, interaction design, information architecture, and user research have become subdisciplines. Technical communication has found a home in the UX team because at its core, user experience design is about facilitating the *communication* between human beings and technology.

UX designers can help documentation professionals succeed by closely partnering with them—if not completely adopting them—in their quest for the ultimate user experience. However, some technical communication professionals may need a mindset shift to succeed in this new role. UX professionals can help them make this transition.

I once wrote an article for the Society for Technical Communication's *Intercom* magazine (May, 1996) that began:

Many, if not most, technical communication professionals waste their time providing services that no one wants or uses. Except in rare cases, they provide little or no value to the organizations that employ them and fail in their efforts to communicate with the users of the products they support.

This may not sound like a great way to encourage technical communicators to rethink their careers, but it caused quite a stir. I stand by it to this day. Companies cannot *write* their way out of a problem they *designed* their way into.

This article spurred several manual writers to transition into more impactful UX writing roles. Some clung to their traditional documentation responsibilities, but many others embraced the opportunity to develop new skills and find more effective ways to contribute to user success.

Imagine shipping a manual with your product with this statement on the first page:

This manual left intentionally blank. If you need assistance, just ask the product.

This is the goal documentation professionals should aspire to. My story in this section describes how I got there; perhaps you can use it to nudge your documentation department in this direction. I'll provide more persuasion techniques in Part 2, *Myth #2: People Read Manuals and Remember Training.*

How Can Documentation Professionals Help UX Succeed?

UX writing is an integral part of successful user experience design. Microcopy—labels, embedded instructions, dialogues, and error messages, and many other information elements—require the expertise of professional writers to ensure clarity and conciseness.

Invite your technical communication colleagues to review the language in your mockups and prototypes. Their eye for detail will spot misspellings, inconsistencies, passive voice, unnecessary words, and a myriad other things that will clean up your design. Every UX designer knows that a simple labeling change is often all that is needed to fix a broken experience. UX writers can help with that.

Make sure language reviews occur before all usability testing and user research sessions; once a user notices a misspelled word, she often becomes distracted and notices little else.

Engage technical communicators in the creation and maintenance of your design system. It's amazing how small differences in language creep into a product portfolio—one product has a button that says "sign in," another says "log in," etc. The technical communicator can compile a glossary of terms to ensure language consistency.

My Story: Working Myself Out of a Job...and Into a Better One

The incident that officially set me on a path from technical writing to UX design occurred during my first job at HP's workstation division. In those days, workstations were paragons of configurability—you could choose from among six different computer models in two different families, run one of three different operating systems on them, connect any of six dozen different peripheral devices to them via fifteen different interface cards, using any one of a hundred different combinations of cables.

Each peripheral device had its own manual; each interface card had its own manual; each computer had its own manual; each operating system had its own manual. Somehow, out of this sea of documentation, the hapless user was supposed to select the peripheral, select and configure an interface card, connect the peripheral to the interface card with the correct cables, and configure the operating system to talk to the peripheral. The number of permutations for any given peripheral installation task was enormous.

Our documentation department's solution was to consolidate all installation instructions into a 700-page manual called the *Peripheral Installation Guide* (fondly known as the *PIG*). It was a complex manual, reflecting the complexity of the tasks that it documented.

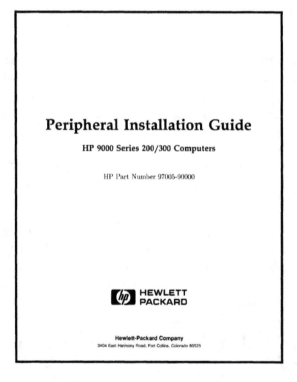

Peripheral Installation Guide

HP 9000 Series 200/300 Computers

HP Part Number 97005-90000

HEWLETT PACKARD

Hewlett-Packard Company
3404 East Harmony Road, Fort Collins, Colorado 80525

Researching and writing the manual was a Herculean feat. As the writer assigned to the project, I prowled the halls of HP in the wee hours of the night in search of peripherals. When I found the one I was looking for, I took it back to my desk to analyze its configuration options, install and test it myself, and then document the procedure when I finally got it to work.

I thought I was providing a valuable service to HP's users with the publication of the *PIG*. It was a high-quality, high-cost manual, designed for quick access with tabs, chapter indexes, and a thorough master index. It had graphics to illustrate spatial tasks like setting interface card switches. It was minimalist and task-oriented, providing only the information needed in the fewest number of words. It was a beautiful manual, a utilitarian masterpiece.

It was a failure.

Follow-up testing and surveys revealed that people couldn't or wouldn't use the *PIG*. Despite my best efforts, our customers cursed and rejected it. How could this be?

I didn't know it then, but the *PIG* and I had fallen victim to technical communication's Big Lie.

Technical Communication's Big Lie

In the 1980s, the technical communication profession operated under a self-induced delusion, a Big Lie. You know the concept of the Big Lie. It's a false idea that, if repeated often enough, everyone begins accepting as truth.

Technical communication's Big Lie was this: People are willing receptacles for the information we produce, and we provide a valuable service without which our customers could not possibly use our products.

I once took a course that asserted documentation quality was measured according to five criteria: accuracy, accessibility, clarity, completeness, and consistency. True enough, but documentation quality misses the point. A document can score high in quality, but still not be effective. The fact that you hit one target doesn't change the fact that you should be aiming at another. We needed a measure, not of quality, but of effectiveness.

Measuring Effectiveness in the *PIG*

The *PIG* was a well-intentioned but ineffective attempt at solving a very complex problem. From the effectiveness perspective, there were several things wrong with it.

The *PIG* documented an irrelevant (Job 2) task. Our customers were not interested in mastering the subtleties of product installation and configuration; they just wanted to print a memo on their printer or scan a picture with their scanner. Users will tolerate a certain amount of irrelevance en route to their true goals, but the *PIG* and the process it documented exceeded the tolerance levels of all but the most technically inclined.

A Better Solution: The Intelligent *PIG*

My analysis of the *PIG* manual led me to a new solution, one that redefined the definition of documentation.

To deliver an effective solution, I needed to reduce the number of irrelevant tasks, decisions, and foreign terms the human being was required to perform and understand.

I had recently coauthored two books on artificial intelligence and had mastered several PC-based expert system applications during my research. Using one of these programs, I built a prototype of the "intelligent *PIG*"—software that contained rules for installation and configuration and automated irrelevant decisions and actions that were difficult for people to perform. It reduced task complexity by over 80%.

I built the prototype to demonstrate how a knowledge-based system could solve problems that a manual couldn't possibly address. By transforming a manual into software, I hoped to show how both solved the same technical communication problem but by different means. One was effective; the other one wasn't.

At the time, the intelligent *PIG* met a lot of resistance. The R&D team felt I had trespassed into their domain, and management worried about supporting the system and keeping it up to date. It took years for the idea to be accepted, but eventually an application similar to the intelligent *PIG* was built.

I did not build it, but I did pioneer the concept. It was my first step away from manual writing toward UX design.

Cultivating Relationships with Professional Services

> Action Plan:
>
> - Attend new customer training sessions and observe audience reactions to product demos.
>
> - Enlist the help of training attendees to provide feedback on new product concepts.
>
> - Give professional services consultants a role in product ideation sessions and invite them to attend design sprints as experts in the voice of the customer.

What Drives a Professional Services Consultant?

Like support and documentation, the professional services team provides users with the information they need to successfully use the company's products. Expensive, complex products rely on professional services to deliver both training at the customer's site and at company training centers, as well as web-based on-demand training.

Profession services consultants measure the effectiveness of their training with post-training surveys, and sometimes with pass/fail rates on knowledge assessments.

How Can UX Help Professional Services Consultants Succeed?

The foundational tenet of product training is that users need to *learn* to use the product. The foundational tenet of UX is that products should deliver promised results with *no learning* required.

The goals of professional services training and the goals of UX design appear to be in conflict. But rather than *teach* the click-by-click operation of the product, professional services would much rather *consult* with customers on best practices in their business domain—helping customers be better educators, better CT technicians, better order processors, etc.

For example, ed-tech company consultants would rather help educators use the product's data visualizations to engage students and parents in meaning conversations. Healthcare imaging consultants would rather help CT technicians reduce the frequency of out-of-focus scans.

Professional services consultants know that customers will forget 90% of product training within a few weeks. As is the case with support and documentation, to be effective how-to training must be integrated into the product at the time and place of need, not delivered in a separate channel.

UX can help with this. As part of your user research, attend training sessions and observe customer reactions. Do attendees look confused during certain parts of product demos? Do they have difficulty following along?

Ask the professional services consultant to give you a few minutes at the end of the training to ask the audience for feedback on the user experience. Record the Q&A if you can (video or audio). Close the session by sending around a signup sheet for attendees who would be willing to review future design concepts.

Back at the office, prototype design solutions for features that caused the most confusion. Ask your professional services consultants to review them, then record video conferencing sessions with training attendees to get their feedback. Share these recordings with your design partners. Emphasize that these are first-time users and that positive first impressions are important for engendering customer loyalty and repeat business.

The UX partnership with professional services empowers consultants to contribute their expertise to the future direction of the company's products. It frees them from teaching routine tasks and affords them time to consult on best practices. It's much more fun for them to show new customers how simple the product is to use rather than to constantly make excuses for its complexity.

How Can Professional Services Consultants Help UX Succeed?

Companies that require classroom training as part of a product purchase usually do so because they believe it's more cost-effective to train users to work with the product than to design the product to work with its users. While this strategy may succeed in the short term and even provide extra revenue, it will eventually fail when a nimbler company with a better understanding of user needs disrupts the market with a simpler product.

Aside from the mutual benefits of using customer training sessions as user research opportunities, professional services consultants can contribute to the user experience by sharing their expertise at design sprints. When product managers and developers become focused solely on features and technology, the stories consultants tell about customer reactions to product complexity can redirect the discussion back to the user experience.

Because consultants are "outsiders" who do not participate directly in product design and development, their insights command greater authority. They are not UX design zealots (like we are ☺), so their impartial reports of customer confusion carry more weight.

My Story: The Serendipity of Feature Simulations

A lot of wins in your career happen by accident.

Because we had an expert prototyper on our UX team, we were able to create—not just static mockups—but high-fidelity interactive simulations of features planned for the upcoming release.

By working several months out of phase with development, we had time to research, create, and iterate these hi-res simulations long before coding would start. We used them in our research efforts at conference expos, inviting attendees to visit our booth, try out a simulation, and give us feedback.

The professional services team staffed our booth and conducted several of these research sessions. To support them, we created a script that told a real-world story along with step-by-step instructions for clicking through the simulation.

The script and simulations serendipitously helped professional services in unanticipated ways. The corporate professional services team created train-the-trainer materials to prepare consultants to train customers on new product features. Because these materials could not be finalized until development of new features was 90% complete, the corporate team was under incredible pressure to complete their work by the release date.

The simulations and scripts enabled the corporate team to produce the train-the-trainer materials much earlier and without waiting for development to complete. As a result, the professional services director became a raving fan of the UX team, and we built a productive and collegial relationship with all consultants in the company.

Cultivating Relationships with Sales

Action Plan:

- Ask your sales team to invite you to upcoming sales calls.

- Express to the customer that you're there to listen and learn how you can make their jobs easier.

- Provide sales with release previews to help them close new deals and generate renewals.

What Drives a Sales Professional?

I'm stating the obvious here, but sales drive a sales professional. Because most of a salesperson's compensation is based on commissions, their ability to sign up new customers, increase renewal rates, and upsell/cross-sell make the difference between a lucrative year and a lean year in their personal finances.

How Can UX Help Sales Professionals Succeed?

Much of a salesperson's success is predicated on their emotional intelligence and skill at building long-term relationships with customers. But there are many success factors outside the salesperson's control—factors where UX can make a difference.

Selling is much easier if the company can:

- Design a product that meets the customer's needs and exceeds their expectations.

- Design a product that demos well and is so easy to use that it sells itself.

- Design a product that delivers a user experience superior to the competition.

In the earlier section on listening tours, I told the story of how a new product (*MENTOR*) was envisioned and how it improved the user experience of the "clicky system" that it replaced. The "clicky system" did not demo well. Customers got lost trying to follow along as the salesperson navigated the maze of features to arrive (finally!) at a result the customer cared about. In contrast, the design of *MENTOR* made simple, compelling sales demos possible.

Ease of learning and out-of-the-box user productivity are competitive differentiators. As discussed in the prior sections, embedding documentation, support, and training into the product itself is a persuasive advantage when compared to competitors that require extensive training, expensive support contracts, and massive documentation sets.

Finally, salespeople absolutely love having UX designers and managers from the corporate office come along on sales visits. When I attended sales calls, the introductions went something like this:

Salesperson: "I'd like to introduce you our product design director and the lead designer for your product. They are here to listen and learn how we can make our product serve you better."

Me: "*Our* job is to make *your* job easier. Your feedback is invaluable to us. The features and enhancements we build in future releases are driven by ideas and feedback from customers like you."

Aside from offering yet another opportunity for user research, your presence on sales calls communicates that the company cares about its users. Customers aren't just an account entry in Salesforce; they are important and deserving of ongoing attention beyond the initial sale. The personal relationships you forge on these visits can make a huge difference in customer renewal rates.

How Can Sales Professionals Help UX Succeed?

Sales can be very helpful in setting up on-site observational research visits. Territory sales VPs usually jump at the chance to arrange research opportunities with their key customers.

Sometimes you'll observe customers using your products in innovative and unexpected ways; at other times you'll feel the customer's pain as they struggle through a clumsy feature. Either way, you'll come away with a trove of ideas for UX enhancements.

If you don't already have relationships with your sales team, ask your product manager to make introductions. Follow up with an email or direct message to schedule a visit. Make sure the product manager and Regional VP are kept informed of your appointments and invite them to come along. If they can't attend, send them a detailed account of your visit with suggestions for things they should follow up on.

My Story: Release Previews

In the last section, I described the happy accident of how our feature simulations contributed to the UX team's relationship with professional services. But that was not the end of the story.

With some refinement, our simulations and scripts were given to sales, enabling them to demo new features several months before release. Instead of tedious PowerPoint pitches, our salespeople could tell an interactive story and demonstrate how our upcoming innovations would solve the customer's big unmet needs.

These high-fidelity simulations looked like the real product. Yes, it can be dangerous to preview features to customers before release, but we were careful to set expectations. Our salespeople informed customers that the simulated features were under development and might not look and work exactly as shown. That didn't matter; customers were excited by the story and unconcerned about the details of look and feel. And because we had validated the feasibility of the simulations with development beforehand, we were confident we could build them.

Release previews were credited with closing several new accounts and generating multiple contract renewals—deals that were sometimes in jeopardy of being lost to our competitors. Long-time customers who thought our products were growing stale stayed with us after seeing the UX innovations that would be coming their way in a few months.

The invention of release previews was one of my UX team's greatest successes.

Cultivating Relationships with Marketing

Action Plan:

- Include marketing on all reviews of customer-facing deliverables to ensure compliance with brand standards.

- Contribute to the corporate blog with stories of user research, corporate UX philosophy, and the story behind breakthrough innovations.

- Build your personal reputation as a UX thought leader by speaking at conferences and publishing on social media.

What Drives a Marketing Professional?

Marketing is driven to enhance the visibility and prominence of the company's products in the marketplace and, in so doing, increase sales.

Marketing creates digital and print collateral such as brochures, product pages on the company website, and social media posts and ads. They issue press releases whenever the company or its leadership receives an industry award. They submit the company's products to industry publications for reviews and publicize wins in product shootouts. They handle the logistics and staffing for the company's presence at trade shows and conference expos.

Marketing defines and maintains the company's brand image. They design color palettes for use in product UIs and marketing collateral, invent product names and logos, and develop marketing campaigns targeted to specific segments that share common needs and interests.

How Can UX Help Marketing Professionals Succeed?

An elegant user experience is a key differentiator in the competitive marketplace and a welcome contributor to any marketing campaign. Features are important, reliable code is important, but the user experience is the thing potential customers get excited about. When a simple product competes in a field of complex competitors, simplicity alone is a marketable innovation. Add unexpected "Wow!" factors like animation, automation, and intelligence, and the product really stands out.

The question is: does your marketing team fully appreciate the value of UX? If you're not directly engaging with them, the answer is probably "no."

You should meet bimonthly with marketing to suggest UX features and activities to showcase on product websites and blogs. Provide marketers with quotes and testimonials from your user research describing how customers are reacting to new design innovations. Breakthrough projects—like those described in Part 4—deserve their own brochure and press release.

UX can contribute to the company's industry eminence and reputation for customer focus by writing stories for the company's blog. Talk about your user research program, design philosophy, and commitment to simplicity.

Develop your own reputation as a UX thought leader by posting on social media and speaking at conferences—your personal prominence enhances the prominence of the company that employs you. And as a product expert, you can assist with product demos, media interviews, and talks at trade shows.

Always ask marketing to review your customer-facing deliverables—including prototypes and release previews—to ensure brand compliance. Engage them throughout the product development lifecycle and keep them abreast of your innovations. Copy them on your release previews and scripts to help them author brochures and other marketing collateral.

How Can Marketing Professionals Help UX Succeed?

In a word: visibility. Regard the marketing department as the UX team's publicist, agent, and promoter. The more marketing advertises your design innovations, the greater your visibility with executive leadership, and the higher the odds of getting your next big innovation initiative approved. In large corporations especially, visibility is critical to your success.

My Story: Branding Innovation

The VP of marketing attended my *MENTOR* pitch to the executive leadership team. Not long after, I received an email invite to meet with him.

I was relatively new to the company and hadn't worked with marketing other than interviewing the VP during my initial listening tour. During that interview,

I got the impression that the UX/Marketing relationship was strained at best. The UX team had not engaged with marketing on brand identity reviews and the designers were resentful when color or font choices had to be changed to comply with marketing's standards.

I had no idea why the VP was reaching out. Were our products out of brand compliance again? I wasn't sure.

We met in the executive conference room. He brought along one of his direct reports and congratulated me on my presentation to the leadership team earlier in the week. Then he got to the point.

"We want to work directly with you to brand 'The Thing' (our *MENTOR* prototype didn't have a real name at this point). We want to contract with the agency that developed our corporate identity to create a unique product name, logo, and color palette for your new product."

I was stunned. Not only was the company going to abandon its original product roadmap to make room for "The Thing," they were willing to pay for a consulting agency to brand it.

Over the coming months, I had regular meetings with the marketing VP and the branding agency. I reviewed and gave feedback on the agency's early concepts and subsequent iterations. I had input into the marketing brochures, press releases, and other collateral they were preparing to launch "The Thing."

When we met with the agency for the final time, they revealed a complete brand package, complete with its new name—*MENTOR* (not it's real name)—and its own logo, font, and color palette.

MENTOR was released with great fanfare a few weeks later. The UX team was the proud progenitor of a thing that started out as a comment from a customer and had evolved into one of the company's greatest innovations.

Occasionally, you get to have your dream job.

Cultivating Relationships with the Executive Leadership Team

> Action Plan:
>
> - On your listening tour, probe for what keeps executives up at night, what they're excited about, and how UX can help them be successful
>
> - Collect and present metrics that prove how UX initiatives contribute to the company's financial performance.
>
> - Launch a high-visibility breakthrough project (details to come in Part 4).

What Drives the ELT?

All executive leadership teams (ELTs) are driven by financial performance. Sales. Revenue. Fixed expenses. EBITA (Earnings before Interest, Taxes, and Amortization). All financial indicators are measured year-over-year and product by product to assess the rate of growth or decline.

For public companies, stock price is a primary measure of financial performance. For private companies with venture capital investors, adherence to approved budgets and return on investment are key performance indicators.

Executive compensation is tied to these financial results. Even more importantly, year-over-year declines in EBITA or market share may cost the executive his or her job.

So, company financial performance is very personal to execs. This explains why they may be risk averse to UX investments that, to you, seem like no-brainers.

How Can UX Help the ELT Succeed?

To get executives to invest in UX, you must walk in the ELT's shoes in the same way you walk in your users' shoes. You must measure success in the same way they measure success.

Passionate arguments for fixing a frustrating user experience will fall on deaf ears unless you put financial justification behind it. It's not that the ELT doesn't appreciate your initiative and zeal. They, too, want to improve their customers' lives. But before they can do this, they must answer to a higher power—the board of directors and investors, and ultimately to the balance sheet.

(At HP in the 1980s—which was one of the most socially-progressive companies I have ever worked for—the #1 corporate objective was profit, and we employees were okay with that. Why? Because without profit, none of the other objectives mattered; we would have neither products nor jobs.)

So how do you sell the value of UX to the executive leadership team?

Answer: One executive at a time.

It helps to get the CEO excited about a UX initiative; then the other execs tend to fall in line. But usually, you must convince each functional leader individually by proving how investing in UX will improve the metrics for which he or she is personally held accountable.

The listening tour is essential. Through these interviews, you will discover what keeps each exec up at night and where they think UX is working well and where it is not. You will discover their current attitudes toward UX, and can assess whether they are your champion, your detractor, or simply indifferent. You will reveal their misconceptions about UX that you will need to disprove through your future actions.

Executive leadership is different from the other roles with whom you work. With the other roles, you collaborate. With executive leadership, you sell, pitch, report, and support. You recruit the ELT to your side with success stories of growth, retention, shareholder value, EBITA, cost reduction, sustainability, equity, and diversity.

Once you understand each executive's metrics, brainstorm how UX can help them. Then establish ways to measure your impact with real data. As you make progress, report back to each leader individually and to the ELT collectively to prove how your initiatives are driving positive change. Use your data, but also tell a story.

How Can the ELT Help UX Succeed?

Like any business function, UX must justify its existence by contributing to a positive balance sheet. This is not hard to prove; UX delivers a mission-critical upside to the company's competitiveness and profitability. It's your job to make executives understand this through stories from user research, support cost reductions, increased customer retention, and all the other datapoints discussed earlier in in this book.

Once UX's contribution to profitability is well documented, then, and only then, is the ELT responsible for providing you with the resources, tools, and investment needed to conduct user research and deliver a world-class, competition-beating user experience for the company.

The fastest route to this state of enlightenment, in which UX infuses every dimension of the corporate culture, is achieved with a breakthrough project, discussed in Part 4.

My Story: UX Metrics that Matter

Earlier I described how a listening tour inspired the invention of a product called *MENTOR*. Because *MENTOR* was born in a pitch to the executive leadership team, it was closely monitored by the entire organization over the course of its design and development.

When *MENTOR* was released, the ELT worked with sales to track metrics on its impact on financial performance. Salespeople were instructed to probe for reasons why existing customers renewed with us, and why new customers selected our product over the competition.

A significant amount of revenue was directly attributed to *MENTOR*. The joke around the company was that the UX team should be given its own sales quota because *MENTOR* was closing so many deals.

The next year, we created a version of *MENTOR* for one of our more mature products. Rather than replacing the existing UI—which would have been prohibitively expensive and potentially disruptive to our customers—*MENTOR* was added as an optional experience layer that sat on top of the legacy product.

Customers had the option of keeping the existing UI or switching to *MENTOR*. We tracked the financial impact of *MENTOR* on customer renewals compared to that of the legacy experience. Data showed that customers who switched to *MENTOR* were significantly more likely to renew their accounts than customers who continued using the legacy UI.

Financial metrics matter. You need to measure them, especially before and after the release of a major UX initiative. Proving that investment in the user experience materially increases revenue and reduces costs is vital to fostering a UX-driven corporate culture.

PART 2.
FOSTERING A UX-DRIVEN CORPORATE CULTURE

Have you ever worked for a company in which you liked and respected your colleagues and yet confronted a corporate culture that was hostile to UX? How is it possible that you can enjoy good working relationships with everyone in the company and still sense a dismissive undercurrent of skepticism and mistrust?

Some attitudes are systemic, not attributable to any one person but are instead deeply infused within the DNA of a company. Persistent myths—about your products, about your customers, and about the mission of UX—trace their origins back to the early 1950s when little if any thought was given to the usability of technology. In all but a few companies, "users" were responsible for adapting to the demands of machines. As UXers, we know this is no longer a viable business strategy, but others in your company may need to be convinced.

The unconscious and unquestioned myths arising from this product-centric view of business persist to this day. They manifest deep in the corporate culture and will remain there until someone exposes their falsity. That's your job: not to evangelize, but to question assumptions, to dispel "self-evident" truths, to steer your company toward a UX-driven culture.

The Solution to Everything

So often, companies measure things but they don't manage them.

Product management measures customer satisfaction and Net Promoter Scores (NPS). Support measures call resolution rates, product returns and warranty costs. Sales and Marketing measure market share, sales closure rates, and retention rates.

All of these metrics are driven by the user experience. But none are diagnostic; none reveal where the experience is broken and needs to be improved.

NPS, for example, asks: how likely are you to recommend our product to a friend or colleague? It determines which customers are Promoters (score 9-10), which are Passives (score 7-8), and which are Detractors (score 0-6) Promoters will tell three people about their experience; detractors will tell nine people.

Net Promoter Scores are useful for *measuring* improvements or declines in customer perception over time, but field research is needed to take the targeted action needed to *manage* the score. NPS without field research leaves changes to the user experience in subsequent releases to guesswork and chance.

To understand and manage the drivers of these metrics, you must observe users in their native environment as they attempt to attain the results your product promised them.

Without user research, you have no foundation for advancing your UX initiatives. Without user research, you're just a zealot standing on a soapbox; your sermons will fall on deaf ears. It's not that others in your company don't find your arguments compelling; perhaps they will. But no action or change in behaviors will occur until you have compelling user research that directly correlates to your corporate-level Objectives and Key Results (OKRs).

Conducting Field Research Without a Research Budget

By now you should understand that user research is essential—not just to inform the design of great user experiences—but as a political tool to engage and recruit patronage from all functional departments in your company.

Don't let the lack of a dedicated research budget prevent you from conducting user research. Even if you have no money for travel to customer sites, and no dedicated staff to conduct research, you can still engage in research activities that will lay the foundation for future investment.

To get started with your research program, work with product management or sales to identify customers that you can talk to. Both teams can provide you with a list of customers whom you can call or email, or they can invite you to participate in customer meetings that are already scheduled.

Set up your research meeting with a conferencing application like Zoom or GoToMeeting and ask participants for permission to record each session. Video clips of users make a much more compelling case for addressing user experience deficiencies than quotes on a PowerPoint slide.

Ask participants to share their screen and walk you through common ways they use your product. If their screens contain personally identifiable information, ask them to click through their scenarios with a demo account that contains dummy data.

User conferences provide another opportunity for research. If your department has a budget for employee training, use these funds to work the booth at a conference expo. Contact the event planner (usually in the marketing department) and offer to help. Set up a table in your company's booth and invite attendees to talk to you about the challenges they face in their jobs. If they are customers, ask about their experience and, if possible, have them show you how they use your product. Offer a gift card as an incentive.

Your call center is another excellent vehicle for user research. Listen in on customer calls to gain valuable insights into user pain points. Offer to send callers an e-gift card if they'd spend a few extra minutes answering your questions.

If you are responsible for designing applications for internal employees, recruiting users for research is easy. Set up a listening tour with users and ask them to demonstrate how they use the application you're researching. Ask them about the last time the application frustrated them. Use an inexpensive screen recording application like Screencast-O-Matic to record your research or just use your Smartphone.

Yeah, But User Research is Useless, Unless...

...you use it to inform design decisions and set the direction of product road-maps. Measurement must be followed by management.

I have worked for companies that, to their credit, invested heavily in field research. Travel expenses to interview and observe customers were never questioned. Everyone in the company was encouraged to visit users and write up their findings. Despite this laudable investment, these findings were largely ignored when needed most—during design discussions and roadmap planning.

Why? Because the research findings were dispersed in hundreds of Word documents and OneNote files. It was too time consuming to comb through all the individual write-ups and extract patterns of pain points and big unmet needs.

User research is wasted unless the notes and video recordings are collected in a repository, tagged, and categorized. Only then can UXers and product managers easily extract and share patterns and insights with the rest of the product team during ideation, design, and roadmap planning meetings.

Aureliuslab.com and Glean.ly offer applications for building, browsing, searching, and categorizing research repositories. Both offer 30-day trials—enough time to assess their value and lobby for a longer subscription if appropriate.

Yes, it can be a lot of effort to import and tag your research, but without this effort, the full value of your findings will never be realized.

My Story: Conducting Research with a Smartphone

I've worked for wealthy companies that invested in high-tech human factors labs with expensive cameras, lighting, recording, and editing equipment. I've worked with companies that spent thousands of dollars on outside agencies to recruit participants and facilitate focus groups.

It's wonderful when you have a substantial research budget. Not only do you get to conduct state-of-the-art research, but these facilities also provide separate observation rooms where executives and colleagues can witness your research firsthand.

However, the most valuable research I've conducted didn't require specialized facilities and equipment. It just required a Smartphone.

Whenever I got the opportunity to speak with users in person—either at customer sites or at conferences—I would ask permission to record our discussion with my Smartphone. Sometimes I used the audio recorder so I could review the conversation when I returned to the office and take notes. When users consented, I used the camera to record video while looking over their shoulders as they navigated through our product and talked aloud about their experience.

Back at the office, my team edited the video recordings into highlights reels. These clips were typically no more than 5 to 10 minutes long and captured the most compelling, entertaining, encouraging, and embarrassing vignettes from the research.

We showed these research highlights at executive leadership meetings, at brown bag lunches, and at the beginning of ideation and design thinking sessions. They served as excellent icebreakers and helped to jump start discussions of UX initiatives we wanted to get approved. More often than not, with this undeniable video evidence from customers, our proposals moved forward.

Dispelling the Seven Deadly Myths of Product Design

Despite all evidence to the contrary, companies with low UX maturity assume beliefs that they have held for decades are still true today. They believe:

- That their products have "users"

- That people read manuals and remember training

- That their product's features are used

- That their products are inherently complex

- That UX is a separate process owned by a separate team

- That feature parity is possible without UX parity

- That they design "products"

Dispelling these myths can be difficult. The message can be hard for people to hear. In some cases, exposing these outmoded beliefs can threaten the existence of entire departments and the people who work in them. You must clearly communicate that you are not questioning your colleagues' competence; you are simply revealing wasted investment and misspent expertise.

As the conveyors of these messages, you must be careful to replace your team-mates' false beliefs with a new compelling purpose…with the assurance that a more meaningful job awaits if they have the courage to accept it.

Myth #1: Our Product Has Users

Scenario 1: I have an old calculator watch. The manufacture thought it was so amazing that they branded it the "Ultimate Watch."

I really like this watch, but every time daylight saving time starts or ends in the U.S., I have to manually change the time. The procedure is complicated, requiring me to follow an illogical sequence of button presses to cycle through its various modes. I can never remember how to do it, so I am compelled to carry around these faded, worn-out instructions in my billfold for the rest of my life:

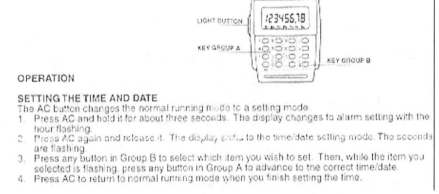

Figure 2. Ultimate Watch Instructions

Note: there are no labels on the watch face that tell you which buttons are in Key Group A and which are in Key Group B.

Scenario 2: I'm writing this book with Microsoft Word. Most of the time, I'm thinking about what I want to say, but occasionally Word does not behave as I expect it to. The spacing between paragraphs is occasionally inconsistent, and no matter what I do—using the format painter, deleting blank lines—I can't get the spacing right. I eventually figure out what's going on, but it takes time and focus away from my writing.

In both scenarios, a subtle change in my identity occurs. In the case of the Ultimate Watch, I stop being a person who wants to know what time it is and I become a *watch user* who is responsible for setting the correct time. In the case of Word, I stop being a writer and am forced to become a *Word user* who is required to understand the subtle mechanics of paragraph formatting.

I don't want to stop what I'm doing and turn my attention to figuring out how to get the product to do what I expect it to do. I don't want to be my product's *user*.

These scenarios seem like such little things to complain about, and they would be, too, if clocks and Word were the only products that make demands of me. But like you, I use dozens of products every day, and each imposes its own set of expectations and requirements on me that must be fulfilled if I am to achieve the results they promised me.

No one wants to be a *user* of your product. This is simply not your customers' goal. People don't want to understand how to *use* a dry cleaner—they want clean clothes. People don't want to understand how to *use* a camera—they want to take pictures. People don't want to understand how to *use* a music app—they want to listen to music.

People don't buy products to be *users*—they buy them to get *results*.

Donald Norman, in *The Design of Everyday Things*, said it perfectly back in 1988:

> *Between us and our machines, we could accomplish anything. People are good at the creative side and interpreting ambiguous information. Machines are good at precise and reliable operation.*
>
> *Unfortunately, this is not the approach engineers have followed in reacting to advances in technology. Instead, they've adopted a machine-centered view of life: machines have certain needs, humans are adaptable. Give the machines priority, technologists' thinking goes, and tailor human operations to fulfill the requirements of machines.*

We, as product designers and engineers, sometimes have trouble understanding this. Our professional lives revolve around the products we create, and we take pride in our creations. But because our products are the focus of our work lives, we extrapolate that they should be the focus of our customers' lives as well. They aren't.

When you introduce yourself to someone, you don't say I'm a Word *user* or I'm an Illustrator *user*. You say I'm a *writer* or I'm a *designer*. You define your identity by your skills and profession. But from Microsoft's and Adobe's narrow perspective, your identity is defined by your relationship with their products. That's what the term "user" implies to me.

Why do I think the user mindset is dangerous? Because it can delude us into thinking our products are the ends and not the means. It deludes us into believing our users will dedicate themselves to mastering whatever complexity our product throws at them. They will happily read its manuals, memorize its complicated workflows, and search its maze of menus and ribbons and dialogs and panels and inspectors for the one button that does what they want the product to do.

But real people—not users—just want to get results. They only become users when the technology forces them to stop focusing on their profession and makes them focus instead on how a product works.

Therein lies the problem. Products are designed for "users," when in fact there *is* no such being. In today's complex and fast-paced world, people don't have the time, patience, or neural capacity to master all the technologies they use every day.

Yet, we have convinced ourselves that we've solved the problem if we strive for product usability, but what is *use-ability*? It's the human being's *ability to use* the product to achieve results. The *user's* ability, not the *product's* ability. Usability places the onus of understanding on the user; as Norman says, the product does what the product does—humans must adapt to it. To truly deliver customer value, we must reverse this attitude and transfer the onus of understanding from the person to the product.

When a person first engages with your product, she should immediately see the first step on the pathway to her result. She should be able to follow that path unimpeded until her result is achieved—without manuals, without training, without calling support.

Can we design such a product? Yes. Is it hard? With our current design frameworks, yes—it's nearly impossible. Are we getting closer than we were forty years ago? Yes. Will we get there? I believe we will. But we have much more work to do. This is why UX is so challenging and so much fun!

How to Dispel this Myth

You dispel the myth of the "user" with research, personas, and journey mapping. Execute these activities correctly and you will introduce your company to the true nature of the people whom they serve. Do them incorrectly and you will produce reams of useless data that will only confuse matters further.

What do you look for when you conduct user research? You look for three things:

- the **results** people are trying to achieve,

- the **actions** they must perform to achieve each result, and

- the **information** they must know to perform each action.

While conducting your observational research, notice whether the information needed to perform an action is unknown. Pay attention to where people look for it, where they find it, and whether they understand it once they find it.

This research provides the data you need to create accurate and meaningful personas rather than fictional characters.

I've never been a fan of personas as a design tool. In my experience, personas are often posted around the office but ignored when making design decisions. Your experience may be different.

However, I *am* a fan of personas as a political tool. Personas can give a name, a face, a profession, and an identity to what were once only generic "users." And if personas capture the results the person wants to achieve rather than made-up demographics, they help design teams focus—not on technology, features, and functions—but on *why* the persona purchased the product. Personas enable you to abandon the word "user" and replace it with the name of a human being who has an identity independent of your product.

After research and personas, journey mapping visualizes the actions and information your product demands of your personas en route to their desired results. It exposes your assumptions about the relevance, findability, and effectiveness of these demands.

What I've just described is not User-Centered Design, but Results-Driven Design. It employs the same tools as UCD but replaces our fixation with the variance among "users" with a focus on the commonality of desired results.

My Story: Getting Rid of the "U" Word (Temporarily)

In my last job at an education technology company, we changed the name of our team from "User Experience Design" to "Experience Design." We stopped referring to our customers as "users" and started calling them what they were:

teachers, administrators, and students. I even posted a declaration of independence from the "U" word in a blog:

It's time to stop using the U word. Calling someone a "user" implies that this person's identity is derived solely from our product, that this person's purpose in life is none other than to *use* this wonderful product we've sold them. It's a subtle complaint I know, but the term has given rise to an entire *cult*ure of user-centered design which I suggest has led us down as many detours as its techno-centric predecessor, the Let's-Build-Something-Fun-And-Throw-It-Over-The-Wall school of product design.

Focusing on the user has inspired many a product team to go forth into the field and collect reams of data on the ages, education levels, genders, zodiac signs, and hair styles of their current customers in the hopes of finding insights that will guide their next design. What usually happens is that the team quickly becomes overwhelmed with data that has absolutely no relevance to the design decisions they need to make. Then, as the schedule closes in around them, they are forced to shelve the data and revert to designing by their instincts.

Instead of focusing on who uses the product, design teams need to focus on Job 1, a term that describes the core goals and activities of our customers. Job 1 for a nurse is caring for and monitoring the condition of a patient. Job 1 for a writer is authoring, editing, and producing documents. Job 1 for a civil engineer is designing bridges and roads. Job 1 for a teacher is teaching grade-level standards in a way that facilitates learning.

I was partly right about getting rid of the "U" word, but I was also partly wrong. I thought that, through this declaration, we could claim that we had no users. But of course, we still did.

Our products had achieved great strides in UX design, but they still required customers to do things they didn't know how to do and know things they didn't already know. We still occasionally forced them to stop being teachers and students and administrators to become *our "users"*—focused not on their jobs but on how to make our products work.

We can't just declare we have no users; we must *earn* the right to retire that word by designing products that allow people to focus on Job 1—100% of the time.

Myth #2: People Read Manuals and Remember Training

In Part 1, I described how documentation professionals can transition from creating hardcopy and online operating instructions to UX writing, and how professional services consultants can be freed from how-to product training to helping customers perform better at their jobs.

I once had a bookcase in my home office that contained manuals from all the software products I used in my job. Taken together, I counted over 11,000 pages of instructions. I then estimated that, in addition to the hardcopy documentation, I was given over 16,000 "pages" of online help. I had read less than 5% of it.

Figure 3. Bookshelf from the Past

I visualized the documentation mentality this way: The user stands on one side of a chasm. The result he wants to achieve is on the other side of the chasm.

In between the user and the result are questions, like:

- How do I control the placement of this picture in my text?

- Where is the Print button?

- What does this error message mean?

- What should I do now?

The user faces a knowledge gap. He lacks the information he needs to answer these questions, cross the chasm, and get the result he wants.

Figure 4. The Knowledge Gap

For the past several decades, product teams have addressed the knowledge gap by building an information bridge across it. This explains why I had over 11,000 pages of documentation on my bookshelf. This is why companies offer hours of live training and recorded webinars to educate their customers. Whenever the product design fails to provide a relevant, findable, and understandable path to results, external documentation, training, and support are deemed the solution.

Figure 5. Bridging the Knowledge Gap with Information

Enter the field of user experience design. UX recognizes that the information bridge—requiring users to read and learn to get answers to their questions—is not a solution. UX understands that users don't want to spend their precious time searching for the information bridge. They don't want to—and can't—retain in memory all the information provided in documentation and training. Reading and learning must not be a prerequisite to achieving promised results.

UX design proposes a different solution to the knowledge gap. Rather than build an information bridge across it, we must *design a solution to close it*.

Figure 6. Closing the Knowledge Gap Through Design

We must face the fact that the information delivery vehicles from forty years ago are not working. Why? People don't want to read, and people can't absorb and retain training.

To be clear, designing products that require no documentation or training is probably not realistic given current design frameworks. Designing products that *embed* answers to questions into the product is the goal. Ideally, the product is designed in a way that eliminates most user questions, but when a question does arise, the answer must be delivered:

- At the moment it is needed,

- In the place it is needed, and

- In the form that best answers the question.

Technical communicators and training professionals already know how to do this. They just need the opportunity to work with the UX team to make it happen.

How to Dispel this Myth

As described in Part 1, the UX team must catalyze the evolution of the company's information delivery strategy by cultivating relationships with documentation and professional services. But as with other UX initiatives, quantifying the cost of this myth starts with support.

Obtain a log of all support calls coming into the call center. Work with your documentation and professional services colleagues to analyze how many calls could have been avoided had the user read the documentation or remembered what they were taught in product training.

Your friends in documentation and training may feel threatened by this analysis. They may suspect your goal is to expose the ineffectiveness of their deliverables and, by extension, prove that their jobs are unnecessary.

Quote Abraham Maslow's Law of the Hammer to them:

> I suppose it is tempting, if the only tool you have is a hammer, to treat everything as if it is a nail.

Reassure them that you goal is to expand their roles in the company with additional, more effective tools. Their current deliverables are essential, but over time they need to move into new channels where they will be found and used.

If you can convince the leaders of the professional services and documentation teams to join your mission, you can then start working on the executive leadership team. Ask for some time in the next leadership meeting, and together with the leaders from the other departments, make your case for a cross-functional pilot project to close the knowledge gap.

Ask these rhetorical questions:

- What is the value of information that is not read?

- What is the value of training that is not retained?

- What is the value of a feature that is not used? (…because no one reads the documentation or remembers their training.)

Then propose that the company's ineffective investments in manuals and training need to be replaced by an integrated omnichannel strategy that delivers information at the place and time of need.

Get approval for a working group, choose a narrow set of problems to solve, and close the knowledge gap by seamlessly integrating documentation and training into the product's UX.

Finally, measure the impact of your pilot project on support call volume and report back to the ELT.

(Interesting bit of history: one of the first instruction manuals was written by James Watt in 1780 to support his invention of the document copier. He glued the instruction sheet to the device, in effect embedding required information into the product where and when it was needed. Why don't we do that today?)

My Story: The Scowling Man at the Back of the Room

In the earlier section on *Cultivating Relationships with Documentation*, I told the story of the *PIG* and how it changed my understanding of the value of documenting problems versus designing solutions.

At dozens of presentations at Society for Technical Communication (STC) conferences, I have challenged technical communicators to repurpose their expertise to UX writing and design. Having worked as a technical writer myself, I try to do this with love, albeit with tough love.

Many writers in the audience understood my message and were inspired to rethink how they practiced their craft. I often taught pre-conference workshops called "How to Work Yourself Out of a Job (and into a Better One)" to provide a game plan for making the transition.

But there was always one guy at the back of the room who scowled at me through my entire presentation. I know what he was thinking: who was I to impugn his life's work and discount the core of his identity?

As you work to dispel this myth at your company, you will likely confront technical communicators, content developers, and trainers who are resistant—and probably hostile—to your message. Listen with empathy and respect, then ask them to apply their craft as editors of the information elements in your designs. Show them how their deliverables can be embedded into the product itself where they are more likely to be found and used. Convince them that you want to increase the scope of their contributions to the company, not reduce it.

At some point, they will have an "Ah-ha!" moment like I did, especially if you invite them to accompany you on customer visits. For me, that moment came when I walked up to a customer's desk and saw my beautiful *PIG* manual on the bookshelf—still shrink-wrapped and unread.

Myth #3: Our Product's Features Are Used

I'm on a site visit, talking to a customer about how we might improve her life with some proposed UX enhancements to our product. We're looking at the application on her computer and she's showing me how she works with it. She's clicking around like crazy.

"It would be so much easier if I could just do XYZ."

I reply, "You *can* do XYZ." I show her how.

"I didn't know you could do that!" she exclaims, incredibly impressed.

This is the story of an underachieving product. The company has invested time, resources, and money to create a feature that few customers know exists and thus have never used.

Ricoh, one of Japan's leading manufacturers of office equipment, surveyed their customers and found that nearly 95% had never used three key features it deliberately built into their machines to make them more appealing. The customers either:

- didn't know these features existed,
- didn't understand utility of the features, or
- didn't know how to use them.

If a feature is buried in the product UI or seems unrelated to the result the user is trying to achieve, the user probably won't discover it. Even if it is found, users won't expend the effort to learn to use it if a first attempt fails. The idea that "if you build it, users will come" is a myth.

The solution, of course, is never build a feature without considering:

- its relevance to the users' desired results,
- its findability,
- and its ease of operation.

In other words, functionality developed without investing in the user experience design is a waste of development time and resources.

How to Dispel this Myth

At the risk of stating the obvious, simpler is better than complex. What is not obvious is *why* so many things are complex and *how* to make things simple.

It's far easier to make complex things. Why? Because complexity just happens. It requires no thought, no planning, no understanding of your customers' needs, and no appreciation for what they want to accomplish.

Simplicity is hard and rare because it takes both the left brain and the right brain, analysis and synthesis, science and art, structure and creativity, decomposition and design.

New products start out simple as minimal viable products (MVPs in the Agile world), but they are not very capable. Over several years and multiple releases, they accrue capability—i.e., features—but do so at the expense of simplicity. Eventually, the effort customers must exert to master the product's complexity exceeds the perceived value they receive from it:

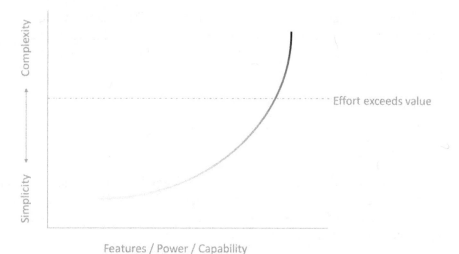

Figure 7. Product Evolution from Simplicity to Complexity

Feedback from the market reveals how complex the product has become. Support calls increase. Sales and retention rates suffer. Net Promoter Scores drop. A simpler product enters the market and steals market share.

In response to these indicators, the product team begins making incremental UX improvements with each release in an attempt to move the product back below the effort/value threshold:

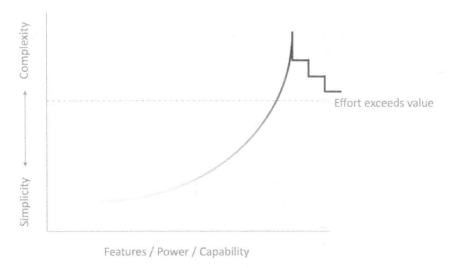

Figure 8. Incremental Simplification

In an attempt to appeal to more casual users, the product team may even surgically remove features to create a new product-lite:

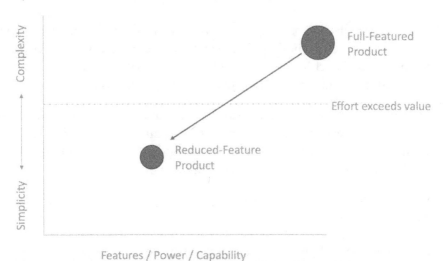

Figure 9. Simplification by Reduction

These efforts may arrest market decline for a while, but eventually the allure of adding new features reverses any incremental gains made in simplifying the experience. Product teams often find it easier to keep bolting new features onto the legacy product rather than admit that the original design framework has exceeded the limits of its usefulness.

What's needed is an entirely new design paradigm, one that retains the product's power and capability while dramatically simplifying the experience of using it:

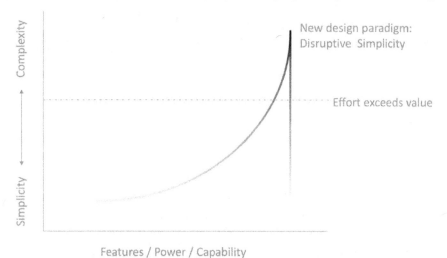

Figure 10. Simplicity by Design

It's difficult to replace an obsolete design framework, but it can—and has—been done. Sometimes it *must* be done. The evolution of software UIs from command lines to GUIs to Direct Manipulation to Voice to VR/AR are examples of replacing an existing design framework with a new, simpler paradigm.

Simplicity by Design is about measuring and reducing what people must do and know to achieve the results our products promised them. It often requires inventing and adopting entirely new design mindsets, models, and methodologies, but as experience designers, that's what we love to do.

To dispel the myth that all your product's features are used, express empathy for the development team:

- During observational research, when you encounter a user who is surprised to learn that the feature she always wanted is already in the product, video record her—ideally at the moment of discovery, but if not, afterward as she explains how thrilled she is to finally find the feature.

- Create a prototype to demonstrate how a UX redesign can surface the feature in the UI to make it easier to find and use.

- Show the video recording and the prototype to the development team and commiserate with them:
"I remember when you spent six weeks building this feature. It's a shame that your elegant solution is buried in the product where no one can find it. But here's an idea that ensures all your hard work isn't wasted."

Like everyone else, developers want their work to be noticed, used, and appreciated. If you can achieve just one success with this tactic, you can repeatedly use it when future stories enter development:

"Remember when the XYZ feature didn't get used until we fixed the UX? The same thing is going to happen with this feature. Let's not waste Julia's excellent work by not spending a little extra time to get the UX right."

My Story: Performance! Performance! Performance!

I once asked a vice president what his top three priorities were for the next release of his high-end workstations. His answer:

- Performance!

- Performance!

- Performance!

Performance was indeed important in his business; the machine with the highest MIPS (millions of instructions per second) rating got a lot of positive press in the technical journals. He was an old-school engineer, trained before "user experience" was even a catchphrase, so it was not surprising that he focused exclusively on technology without consideration for the people who used it.

I asked him: "If performance is our only priority, why then are competitor's slower machines outselling our hotrods?"

I argued that the performance bottleneck was not with our computers, but with our users. The complexity of installation, configuration, and operation were grinding *user* performance to a crawl.

I told him the story of the Xerox 8200 copier and how, in some cases, top-of-the-line technology can impede success. In 1980, the Xerox 8200 copier was the first product failure in Xerox history, yet it was the most technologically advanced machine the company had ever built. They piled on so many features that users who just wanted to enter the number of copies and press Start were overwhelmed.

Arnold Wasserman, leader of the Industrial Design/Human Factors Design Center and Xerox PARC, described it this way:

> *Xerox strategy at that time was to grow by expanding the use of collating, enlarging, reducing, and other fancy features. The only problem was that no one paid attention to the human interface—to the user. People had to wade through buttons and visual noise and manuals for all features, including the most frequently used one, copying a page or two. Old customers abandoned Xerox for simpler machines and their market share plummeted.*

From an engineering standpoint, Xerox had designed their most innovative product ever. From a customer standpoint, Xerox lost its mind.

I'd like to say that my VP grokked what I was telling him. Later that year, I proposed a UX initiative to simplify the workstation user experience. I made my case, showed him a prototype, and hoped for a green light. He congratulated me on my initiative, but then invoked the Wizard of Oz Syndrome, described in Part 4.

My initiative never got off the ground, but years later the VP began referring to our workstations as "a thousand parts flying in close formation." The importance of UX was starting to sink in.

Myth #4: Our Product's Domain is Inherently Complex

Sometimes companies recognize that their products are difficult to use, but they don't see it as a problem. They believe their business domain is inherently complex and therefore their products cannot be simplified. Furthermore, their technically-savvy and highly-educated customers—scientists, technicians, and engineers—love a good challenge. A simpler product would insult their intelligence.

But smart people are not all smart about the same things, nor do they want to be, nor should they be.

An expert accountant might design a company's time and expense reporting system in a way that makes perfect sense to another expert accountant, but small business owners will find the myriad accounting codes unnecessarily complex.

An expert technologist might design a cell phone that has all the latest features and functionality, but the Nobel-Prize-winning chemist who buys it just wants to make a phone call.

This is the Smart People Paradox: to design and build advanced technology for complex domains, companies need smart people. But these same smart people often insist on adding complexity to the user experience—complexity that is second nature to them—but that only serves to confuse users and hinder the company's success.

Every technological innovation is complex when first invented. Look at old computers, old telephones—old *anything*—and you'll see a mass of wires and jury-rigged parts that no one could use without considerable effort and training. As the product matures, the raw technology disappears under increasingly simplified layers of the user interface. The "inherent complexity" turns out to be not so inherent after all, and the product's increasing simplicity allows the underlying technology to be used in ways the original inventors never envisioned.

Early computers, for example, were very complex. ENIAC, an early computer developed to calculate missile trajectories during World War II, occupied 1800 square feet (167 square meters) of floor space and weighed 30 tons. A couple of very smart people—John Mauchly and J. Presper Eckert—invented ENIAC as a complex solution to a complex problem. Scores very smart women (called "human computers") were enlisted to operate it.

Figure 11. ENIAC and Computing Complexity

These early computer pioneers never envisioned their invention would spread beyond government and academia. Thomas Watson, founder of IBM, reportedly said, "I think there is a world market for maybe *five* computers." A writer for *Popular Mechanics* magazine in 1949 expressed what at the time was incredible vision, predicting that computers in the future might weigh *only* 1.5 tons.

Implicit in this reasoning is the assumption that products will never evolve much past their current design. The inventors and operators of ENIAC were brilliant engineers, fully immersed in the technical problems they had to solve. Yet it is often this brilliance that blinds technologists to the possible extensions of their inventions beyond their original use. Wouldn't they be shocked today to see how their inherently complex creations have evolved?

Figure 12. Product Evolution from Complexity Toward Simplicity

Problems may be complex. The underlying technologies that solve these problems may be complex. But to assume that a product is, and always will be, complex because it is constructed from complex technology to solve complex problems is to fundamentally misunderstand product evolution.

While it's true some portion of current customer base may be insulted (or threatened) by simplicity, you will open entirely new and much larger markets by making your technology accessible to more people. Contrary to the prevailing wisdom in technology-centered companies, most customers welcome simplification.

How to Dispel this Myth

To dispel the myth of inherent complexity, ask WWAD?—What Would Alexa Do? If your inherently complex product had an intelligent voice interface, how would your users interact with it?

For example, I might tell Adobe Photoshop:

> *Alexa, remove the background from this photo and save it with a file size of less than one megabyte.*

Decompose this statement. There are two actions in this command—*remove* and *save.* Also provided are the bits of information required to perform each action—*background* and *file size < 1mbyte.* Alexa might need to ask for additional clarification, such as "What should I name the file?" but this is information the user can easily provide.

Notice that the user would *not* phrase this command as:

> *Alexa, right-click the Object Selection Tool in the toolbar on the left side of the screen and choose the third option named Quick Selection Tool and click at various points to surround the foreground image or click Select Subject in the upper Options menu bar and use Quick Mask mode to correct any imperfections and then click Layer via Copy and....*

You get the idea. The Alexa command requires only the user's desired result and the *relevant* actions and information required to achieve it. Comparing it to the Adobe design framework exposes all the *irrelevant* actions and information—menus and panels and buttons and settings and terminology— foisted upon users by the current, "inherently complex," design.

The purpose of this thought experiment is not to encourage product teams to craft an intelligent voice interface. The purpose is to inspire product teams to rethink their assumptions about what the user *must* do and know to achieve promised results—to break through the myth of inherent complexity. Is there a way to make the user's desired result easier to accomplish? Be willing to ask this question rather than assume no better answer is possible.

Never stop asking, "What's next?"

One final bit of advice: Your quest for simplicity will be much easier if you and your colleagues speak the customer's language throughout the product development process. The internal language a corporation uses is often the culprit for poor design.

I once worked with a company that had a reputation for high UX maturity but still allowed internal marketing and technical language to creep into the design of a new product. Vague terms like *clusters, trees, targets,* and *probes*—language understood by everyone on the development team—confused users when the prototype was field tested. The team had to go back to the drawing board and scrub out all the company-speak.

Users should never have to ask, "What does this mean?" If your corporate language matches the language of your users, you can avoid this common source of frustration.

My Story: Maybe It Is Rocket Science?

Whenever I contend to product development teams that simplicity represents the pinnacle of product evolution, some guy always raises his hand, smiles condescendingly, and says, "You don't understand. Maybe you can simplify a cell phone or a digital camera, but we make gene-mapping machines. Our products are inherently complex."

"Yeah," agrees one of his colleagues. "Our customers are Ph.Ds. They'd be offended if we 'dumbed down' the user interface and made our products easier to use."

Whenever I hear this, I smile and tell them that their product is not inherently complex, it's just technologically immature. Their argument is a cop out. Cobbling together components into a complex technical solution is the easy part; designing it so that real people can use it is the hard problem.

One of my colleagues worked for a company that sold high-end machines for testing printed circuit boards. A simplification advocate, he was always running up against the twin notions of inherent complexity and insulting simplicity. "Yes, our products may be complex," the other engineers admitted, "but they're not rocket science."

One day, he and his fellow engineers got the opportunity to visit a major customer—Los Alamos National Laboratory—to observe how their products were being used in the real world. The "not rocket science" argument was squelched forever when many of the users they observed were indeed rocket scientists, and even they found the board testers hard to use. In fact, over eighty percent of these rocket scientists said they had less time than ever to learn how to use their test equipment, and that their equipment needed to be significantly less complex and easier to use.

The lesson they learned that day, and the lesson every technology-centered company needs to learn, is that customers want to focus on their jobs, not on their tools. Product teams may think their users are impressed by complexity, but simplicity is even more impressive and considerably more rare.

Myth #5: UX is a Separate Process Owned by a Separate Team

UX professionals often proclaim that the user experience *is* the product. If this is true—and I believe it is—then UX is everybody's job. While every department in the company has its distinct and specialized skillsets, *responsibility* for the user experience pervades every function in the company.

Functional silos account for the myth that UX is owned and operated by a separate team. Rooted in the business principles of the Industrial age, employees are given a scoping, a ranking, a job description, a position plan, and a place in the organizational caste system. Boundaries are drawn around departments. Any attempted contribution outside of these established norms is viewed as a territorial trespass.

Experience design is—or can be—the great uniter of silos. Every department provides an experience to the company's customers and users. The accumulated effect of these experiences determines whether the company will grow or shrink its customer base.

At the turn of this century, the concept of Total Customer Experience (TCE) gained traction. Rather than narrowly defining CX/UX as a product design discipline, TCE expanded the notion of experience to the encompass the entire lifecycle of the company's relationship with its customers.

The stages of TCE were often arranged along a timeline:

Figure 13. Total Customer Experience (TCE) Timeline Circa 2000

While a timeline is not an accurate depiction of the TCE—the middle stages of Achieve, Achieve More, Troubleshoot, and Maintain do not conform to a linear sequence—it does provide a useful visualization of the high-level user goals that arise over the life of the user-product relationship—beginning with "I want to choose…" and ending with "I want to replace…"—then starting all over again.

Each stage has a set of touchpoints where the customer and the company interact, i.e., where the company provides an experience for its customers. For example, during the Choose experience, you might assume the primary touchpoints are between the potential customer and the company's marketing and sales teams. However, the work of every department affects the potential customer's experience—and ultimately her purchase decision—at this stage:

- Does the product do what I want it to do? (Product Management, Development)

- Is the product easy to use? (UX)

- Does the company stand behind its products? (Support, Documentation, Professional services)

- Is the product reliable? (QA)

- Will the company be around in the long-term? (ELT)

Even though every department *delivers* an experience (whether they know it or not), UX is generally the only group that knows how to *design* them. This is where your UX team can make its most impactful contribution to your company. Through ongoing engagements with each functional area, the mindsets and methodologies rooted in UX DesignOps and ReOps will spread and permeate the entire organization, culminating over time in a mature UX-driven corporate culture.

How to Dispel this Myth

In Part 1, I described how to recruit allies to the UX cause by contributing to each department's success metrics. Often these metrics are in conflict—one team is accountable for on-time delivery, while another is accountable for product quality, while another is accountable for sticking to the budget. Or, as the Project Management Triangle says: Fast, Good, or Cheap—pick two.

If you follow the guidance in Part 1, your partners will learn to balance their metrics with those of their colleagues. Eventually, all will embrace a common superseding goal:

Deliver the best possible user experience from first customer contact through to product replacement.

This shared goal, combined with empathy for the user and for each other, will reduce conflict, streamline decision making, and broaden everyone's perspectives to include those of other roles.

Realistically, you're not going to dissolve functional silos in your organization, nor should you. Each functional area deserves its own unique microculture that serves the members of that team (more about this in Part 3). The Four-Legged Stool of product design—the UX lead, product management lead, product owner, and development lead—comprise the core of the product team, but all other functional areas need to participate as well—not just on the periphery, but as indispensable members.

Team members, regardless of their "home" department, must feel free to contribute their expertise in any way that excites them. By encouraging ideas from anyone for anything, you are more likely to surface innovations that would otherwise remain buried.

Static roles must also go; the responsibilities of team members can change from week to week depending on the activities the team is pursuing and the skills each team member can offer. In addition to being expert coders, marketers, designers, or writers, everyone must become expert in understanding the results your users want to achieve.

How do you soften the boundaries between silos? Once again, it's The Solution to Everything: invite members from every department to participate in user research. Post research visit schedules on the company intranet and encourage people to sign up for slots. (Limit each away team to three or four people though—you don't want to overwhelm your research subjects with a large crowd.) Reassemble the teams back at the office to debrief, discuss, and document what they observed.

By giving every member of the extended product team the opportunity to observe and interview users, you establish a foundation of user empathy across all functions and lay the groundwork for insights from everyone regardless of their job description.

My Story: Giving and Taking Credit

Angie (not her real name) was a UX designer that I hired right out of college. After a year of experience, she was ready to take on one of the most challenging projects our team had ever faced.

We had recently "merged" with another company (it was really an acquisition) and the integration of the two cultures had not gone smoothly. Several employees left, and those who remained harbored resentment for being force-fit into the parent company's processes and procedures.

I assigned Angie as the sole UX designer for the acquired division's flagship product. This division had no prior experience working with UX; before the merger, the UI design had been development's responsibility. Angie faced an uphill battle just getting the engineers to accept and respect her role on the product team. She also worked from a remote office, which further exacerbated the situation.

The product Angie was assigned to was very successful. It had dominated its market for several years but more recently was showing its age. As often happens with products that mature without the benefit of UX attention, it had outgrown its original design framework. New features were bolted on wherever the engineers could find a place to put them. After fifteen years of releases, it had become bloated and difficult to use.

Angie's project initially progressed as expected. She submitted her mockups to the development team and the sprints began without incident.

One Friday afternoon midway into the project, I met with Angie and asked her how everything was going. I could sense she was conflicted about something.

She told me that one of the developers had deviated from her submitted design and had instead constructed his own concept.

Angie showed me her design and the one the developer had proposed. The developer's design was better, and Angie knew it. Her confidence had taken a hit and she was worried that her career was at risk. After all, if a developer could "do her job" then why was she even here?

I told her that others may propose good UX design ideas, but that she still "owned" UX responsibility. The only metric that mattered was whether the final design delivered the best possible user experience. If it did, she would get credit for leading the UX effort, regardless of whether others may have contributed to it. In fact, as her manager, I would give her *more* credit for having the maturity to accept a better design from outside the UX team rather than insist that her own design must best all others.

The work of a UX designer naturally catalyzes ideas from the rest of the product team. Often these ideas are superior to the original idea that inspired them. This doesn't mean the UX designer has failed. Quite the contrary, if the designer's work has stimulated her teammates to think deeply about the user experience, she has fulfilled her mission.

Myth #6: Feature Parity is a Winning Product Strategy

Product managers and executives believe maintaining "parity" with the competition is essential to sustaining a viable business. If they can check all the features their competitors check in a product comparison chart, they will win at least an equal portion of market share.

Feature	Our Product	Competitor 1	Competitor 2	Competitor 3
Feature A	✓	✓	✓	
Feature B	✓	✓		✓
Feature C	✓	✓	✓	✓
Feature D	✓	✓	✓	
Feature E	✓	✓		✓

Figure 14. Product Comparison Chart

Feature parity is important but insufficient. When product managers speak of parity, rarely do they consider UX. It's one thing to tell potential customers that we have all the features our competitors do, but another to say our features are easier to use and will make you more productive.

Feature parity creates a state of equilibrium where customers migrate from one company to another in search of a decent experience. No brand loyalty is earned, and all companies incur the costs of constant customer turnover.

When companies focus solely on checking the boxes in a feature comparison chart, three outcomes are possible:

- You maintain parity with your competitors, and they maintain parity with you. Your business next year will be like business this year. This is as good as it gets.

- You maintain parity with your competitors, but a new company enters the market with a product that delivers the same features *and* a superior user experience. You and your competitors try to maintain market share, but it's too late. You all lose.

- *You* develop the product with all the same features but with a breakout experience, upset competitive parity, and dominate the market.

Which scenario is most likely at your company? Probably #2 unless someone takes the initiative to start advocating for #3. Maybe you?

How to Dispel this Myth

UX parity (or superiority) cannot be conveyed by checkmarks in a product comparison chart. It requires a different form of messaging.

Work with product management to conduct a competitive analysis. While the product manager analyzes feature parity, the UX team analyzes the experience of using each feature.

If you have access to your competitor's product, walk through the workflows required to produce the same results your product delivers. If you can't get access to the competitor's product, review the step-by-step instructions in the product's documentation, often available on their support website. You may also find customer-created training videos of your competitor's products on YouTube.

When co-presenting your competitive analysis to the executive team, your product manager can capture feature parity in a comparison chart, but the UX analysis requires a journey map or, better yet, a live demo (or video clip) combined with a simplicity scorecard.

I'll go into more detail on UX analysis and simplicity scorecards in Volume 2: *Operations*, but for now compare the following:

- Number of actions (e.g., clicks) required to achieve results with a feature.

- Itemization of the information required to perform all actions and the findability of that information.

- Terminology and labeling that may confuse a typical user.

- Estimated Time-To-Result (get out your stopwatch).

Provide your sales and marketing teams with the feature and UX competitive analyses. Provide them with a script of responses to use when a potential customer asks why they should buy your product over a competitor's.

There's one more little trick to use if your competitor delivers a user experience superior to yours, but you can use it only once:

- Build a prototype of your vision of the ideal experience.

- When reporting your competitor analysis to the executive leadership team, demo your prototype but...

- ...put your competitor's logo on it!

Wait for the shock and awe and let them worry for a little while, then slowly dissolve the competitor's logo into your own. Suggest how this concept would be a competition killer if you build it now before your competitors do.

My Story: We're No Worse than the Competition

I once made a pitch to a product manager to convince him to include an important UX initiative in the product roadmap. I thought it was a compelling presentation, replete with data and a prototype of the new and improved experience. He listened politely and then remarked:

"As long as we're no worse than the competition, we don't need to invest in improving our UX."

I learned two things from this:

- UX presentations that attempt to educate and excite non-UX colleagues usually don't produce the desired change.

- Parity with—i.e., being just as bad as—the competition can work against you.

At this point in my career, I did not account for the metrics the product manager was responsible for. He had a budget he could not exceed and, given all the competing ways to spend that budget, UX priorities were low on his list.

Looking at my proposal through his eyes, his decision made sense. He believed he would not lose any customers because of a mediocre user experience, and I had not proven otherwise.

Had I known then what I know now, I would have let our users make the pitch for me. I am ashamed to admit that I conducted no user research while employed at this company. Had I done so, I would have recorded videos of frustrated users as they struggled to get results with our product. I would have collected stories from our sales team describing why users defected to our competitors. I would have called attention to users' confused and exasperated reactions during demos in new product training sessions.

Back then, I was reasonably competent in UX design, but a novice in UX politics. The former is not enough; to get stuff done, you must master the latter, too.

Myth #7: We Design Products

When I pick up the remote control for my home theater, I have a result I want to achieve. Perhaps the phone is ringing, and I want to mute the sound. Perhaps I want to watch a new Blu-ray that I just bought. Perhaps I'm not getting surround sound and I want to figure out why. In any case, I'm results driven.

The same is true when I use a service, like a dry cleaner, a shipping service, or a banking app. I want my clothes to be clean. I want to ship something to my son in college and ensure it arrives by Tuesday. I want to deposit a check into my checking account.

The same is true when I follow a process at work. I want to post a job requisition to hire a new employee. I need to order a new software application. I need to update my tax withholding. The company has processes in place that I am supposed to follow to achieve each of these results.

If I can't mute the sound, or watch my Blu-ray, or restore surround sound, or if my clothes don't come back clean, or if my son doesn't receive the shipment on Tuesday, or my deposit into my bank account doesn't register, or my job requisition doesn't get posted, or my new software purchase isn't approved, or my tax withholding isn't adjusted—in other words, if I don't get the result I'm after—I will consider the product, service, or process a failure. I'll be angry, frustrated, and discouraged. If I have a choice, I may decide I don't have the time or desire to try again. I'll find another way.

Even if I do eventually achieve the result I want, but the trial and error experience took too much time and effort, my dissatisfaction with the product, service, or process will erode my loyalty. When I seek this result again, I will try to find an alternative to the product, service or process I used the last time.

The point is this: People don't buy products, they buy results.

When a user fails or struggles to achieve a result with a product, it doesn't mean that the product is incapable of delivering the result. The result may indeed be *possible*. But the requirements that the user must satisfy to achieve the result exceed her capabilities and tolerance. This is where the user experience enters the picture.

The user experience comprises the actions the user must perform and the information the user must know to achieve a given result. Results can only be achieved if the product *and* the user can each perform the functional responsibilities assigned to them by the product design.

So, you do *not* design products; you design a system of interacting components for achieving results. The user is one of the components in this Results System. If you are only designing the product component, you're only designing part of the system.

Imagine you're the dealer in a card game. The players sitting around the table are the components in the Results System: software components, hardware components…and the user, the human component. Why must you include the human component in the game? Because, just like the software and hardware, the human being must perform functions—like tapping buttons and entering information—that are required for the system to work.

Now deal the cards. Each card in the deck represents a function that must be performed for the Results System to work. Some cards are dealt to the data center. Some are dealt to the graphics processor. Some are dealt to cloud services. And some are dealt to the user. Once the cards are distributed, it's the product team's job to ensure that each component can reliably execute the function cards that you dealt to it.

But sometimes, after development is underway, the product team looks at one of the function cards assigned to the software component and decides it's going to take too long or be too difficult to implement. So, what does the product team do? They call for a re-deal. They remove the function card from the software's stack of cards and reassign it to the user. Just include instructions for the function in the documentation, they say. Problem solved.

Would you assign a function to your product that exceeds its system requirements? Would make function calls to a stored procedure that you know does not exist? Would you tolerate writing code that, when needed, took minutes or hours to load? Would you call a function without supplying required parameters? Of course you wouldn't. Yet product teams do this to the human component all the time.

This doesn't mean the human component isn't required to do things; it just means that the things the user component must do must be *relevant*—i.e., things the user wants to do and is good at. I don't want to buy a TV that decides which channel I should watch; choosing channels is relevant and my responsibility and I want to keep it that way. But I don't see why I should have to understand the difference between S-Video and Component Video or remember to set the video input to COMP when I want to watch a Blu-ray movie but set it to VID2 when I want to watch the evening news.

Once you accept that your company designs and sells Results Systems and not just products, you will start to recognize new opportunities and new competitive threats.

Western Union, for example, had the opportunity to acquire the Bell telephone patent but turned it down because they narrowly defined themselves as a "telegraph company." They were too product-centric to recognize the telephone as a viable next-generation product, one that delivered the same result as the telegraph but with a superior user experience (no Morse code required).

Consider Netflix versus Blockbuster. Both were Results Systems for watching movies, but Netflix removed the irrelevant user requirements of driving to the video store and paying late fees, then later eliminated the wait for movies to be delivered by mail. Blockbuster was positioned to do the same. Why didn't they?

Product design and service design are the same thing because products and services are simply different paths to the same result, distinguished only by the experience they provide. A customer can purchase a *product* (an HP copier) to copy a manuscript, or she can purchase a *service* (from the UPS store) to achieve the same result. HP and UPS are, in fact, competitors, at least in some markets and for some results. Likewise, Delta Airlines competes with Zoom and MS Teams for dollars spent on business meetings.

Yet most companies, to their peril, only look at *direct* competitors: Delta Airlines competes with Singapore Airlines; HP competes with Epson. Unless companies awaken to the realities of business in the Experience Age, they risk being blindsided by a competitor they didn't see coming.

How to Dispel This Myth (and Save Your Company)

If your company has embraced the Agile development methodology, you're already expressing results as user stories. For example, if you're building a banking app, you might include this story in your backlog:

As an account holder, I want to deposit a check into my checking account using my Smartphone.

This story expresses a result a user wants to achieve. In Agile, chances are your Four-Legged Stool—the product manager, the lead UX designer, the product owner, and the lead developer—already think of your product as a Results System and didn't know it.

What you're probably *not* doing is explicitly capturing and analyzing the feasibility of the functional responsibilities you have unconsciously assigned to the user component. These user requirements—requirements the product makes of the user, *not* the requirements the user makes of the product—will determine the success or failure of your product in the marketplace.

To capture your product's user requirements, list all the *actions* the user must take and all the *information* the user must know to achieve the result in your story. For example:

Result: Deposit a check into my checking account.

What the user must do (actions)	What the user must know (information)
Launch the banking app	Location of banking app on the Smartphone screens; appearance of the app icon
Enter username and password	Username and password; location and label of the Done/Enter button.
Write "For online deposit only" on the back of the check	These exact words must be written on back of check
Enter the check amount.	Check amount and location and label of the field
Take a picture of the front of the check	Orientation of the check in camera screen and contrast with the background
Take a picture of the back of the check	Orientation of the check in camera screen and contrast with the background
Confirm deposit	Accuracy of deposit summary info and label of the Confirm Deposit button
Verify deposit was made	How to navigate to the list of transactions

Figure 15. Action and Information User Requirements

Next, ask the following questions:

- Are the action and information requirements **relevant** to the result?

- Are the action and information requirements **findable?**

- Are the action and information requirements, once found, **effective?**

Note: findability and effectiveness include accessibility—designing for people with different abilities.

Taking the second user requirement as an example:

- Are the username and password **relevant** to the result?

   No, they may be *required* for the current design to work, but they are not *relevant,* just like Blockbuster late fees were not relevant to watching a movie and Morse code was not relevant to communicating with a remote friend. Security is relevant, but this method of achieving security is not.

- Are the username and password **findable?**

   Not very, especially if the user changes her password frequently. She probably keeps a record of her passwords someplace, but it may be a hassle to find it.

- Are the username and password, once found, **effective?**

   The user probably can successfully enter the username and password, meaning the information is effective once found.

Once you've performed this quick analysis, you can see where improvements to the user experience can be made. Passwords are not relevant or very findable. How else can we achieve security? How about biometrics, like a fingerprint reader? Fingers are usually findable.

This analysis helps the product team identify elements of the proposed user experience that can be simplified or eliminated altogether. It shortens and straightens the user's road to results and decreases the likelihood that your Results System will fail due to a "faulty" user component.

My Story: The Accidental Wow!

We built a simulation for a conference expo to demonstrate and research the design of new features coming in our next release. Our previous research had shown that our users wanted to group objects and apply the same action to every member of the group rather than acting on each object one at a time. This made sense; a grouping feature would be a great time saver.

Our challenge for the prototype was how to *quickly* demonstrate the process of creating a group. People who attend expos don't want to spend a lot of time in any one booth, so we needed a way to speed up the grouping feature for demo purposes.

In our prototype, objects were represented as cards. Users could drag cards into groups based on similar attributes. For example, you could drag the object cards in the left-hand column into the appropriate attribute columns on the right:

Cards		Mammals	Fish	Reptiles
Dog				
Guppy				
Alligator				
Shark				
Camel				
Rabbit				
Lizard				

Figure 16. Objects to be Grouped

Manually dragging the cards would take a lot of time, so for our demo we created an invisible button that animated the movement of the cards into the attribute columns. In just a couple of seconds, the groups were created:

Mammals	Fish	Reptiles
Dog	Guppy	Alligator
Camel	Shark	Lizard
Rabbit		

Figure 17. Result of Auto-Grouping

As soon as the cards started flying around and landing in attribute columns, conference attendees were shouting "Wow! Auto-grouping! That's fantastic! This will save me so much time!"

In the real product, the cards were people, not animals, and the attributes reflected each person's performance on a task. Because the product stored the attributes of each person, the cards could indeed be auto-grouped, relieving the user of the time-consuming task of grouping them manually. The result—group these people based on common attributes—could be achieved with a single click.

From the Results System perspective, we had inadvertently transferred responsibility for a tedious and irrelevant function from the user to the product.

What was originally conceived as a time-saving step in the demo became a "must" feature in the product. It wasn't an easy feature to code, but development found a way to build it and it became a Wow! selling point that differentiated our product from its competitors.

PART 3. DESIGNING A SUPPORTIVE UX MICROCULTURE

As businesses transition from the Information Age into the Experience Age, rapid innovation is essential to success. In-house creative teams with their deep knowledge of customers and comprehensive understanding of the company's business domain are poised to drive innovation, but their potential is often squandered by outmoded management attitudes, leadership styles, and HR policies.

Managing creatives as you would other functional roles is a formula for slow death in today's dynamic marketplace. The solution? Turn your creative teams loose to visualize your company's vision and invent fresh solutions to wicked-hard design problems that fulfill customers' big unmet needs.

To do this, we need to rethink creative team leadership. Running a company's creative team requires an approach that is vastly different from managing other teams. Unlike other professions in which processes and deliverables are clearly defined, creative people conjure their deliverables out of the ether using processes that even they don't fully understand. Managing them as you would other employees will only stifle their creativity, reduce their capacity for innovation, and ultimately lead to high turnover and a loss of valuable institutional knowledge.

I've led creative teams (and they have led me) for over three decades. In this part of the book, I'll share effective ways to craft an inspirational UX microculture in which creatives can perform to their full potential. Some of the strategies are obvious. Others are counterintuitive. Still others are downright dangerous, especially if you work for a company that still believes employees should sit in a cubicle and stare at a screen for eight hours a day.

The Demise of the Mockup Factory

Today, virtually every organization has embraced some flavor of Agile development principles and practices. Many improvements in efficiency, quality, and delivery have resulted. But Agile is not perfect. It's not the final stage in the evolution of development strategies above which no replacement process can be conceived. Like all corporate religions (remember Six Sigma?), it too will be replaced by some new new thing.

Business practices fall out of favor when true believers try to force-fit them into situations where they don't make sense. As a long-time practitioner of Human-Centered Design (and more recently, Design Thinking and Design Sprints), I know that prescribed multi-step processes are not always pragmatic given the composition and culture of an enterprise and the speed and pressures forced upon it by a global economy.

In my experience with Agile, the insistence on continuous delivery of valuable software compresses the time required for design iterations. Agile principles supposedly welcome revisions late in the development cycle, but while requirements may change, modifications to the experience design are often vehemently resisted.

Because of this resistance to late design discoveries, many experience design groups devolve into mockup factories—one-and-done assembly lines—in order to keep the Agile machine running at full speed. If a designer wants to make a change after a mockup has been handed off to development—resulting from additional research, usability testing, or just an "Ah-Ha!" breakthrough in her understanding of the design problem—she is often faulted for not delivering the perfected design the first time.

Of course, UX designers cannot iterate indefinitely. Products do need to ship. There are ways to accelerate the research-design-test-learn cycle practiced by UX teams. But we must also find better ways to accommodate creative inspiration and design breakthroughs in our Agile processes.

Innovation requires inspiration, iteration, dogged determination, deep analysis, collaboration, and continuous discovery—all of which cannot always be time-boxed in a sprint roadmap. And in today's ultra-competitive marketplace in which start-ups can disrupt established players, companies must innovate or die.

Recruiting allies to your cause and dispelling the myths of product design will make it easier to balance Agile's need for speed with UX's need for exploration and experimentation. But until your corporate culture climbs up UX maturity scale, you will need to construct a localized work environment in which your UX team can thrive.

Following are suggestions for designing a supportive UX microculture, one that liberates designers and researchers to do their best work and maximizes their contribution to the organization.

Time

It's 2pm on a Wednesday afternoon. You've had a productive morning, but you've been beating your head against the wall for a couple of hours trying to find an innovative solution to a wicked-hard design problem and you're not getting anywhere. You have three hours to go before it's time to go home and you're expected to sit at your desk in your 10x10 cubicle, stare at the screen, and make sure your presence indicator shines green until quittin' time. That's what you're paid for. Eight hours, not five.

If you manage a creative team, I hope you don't subscribe to this "butts in seats for eight hours a day" philosophy. But I have seen it happen, particularly when the leadership of a UX team is transferred to a product management or development director/VP who has never worked as a UX designer.

There's an activity called "Crazy 8s" on Tuesday's agenda in *Sprint: How to Solve Big Problems and Test New Ideas in Just Five Days* by Jake Knapp. In this exercise, participants have eight minutes to sketch eight solutions to a design problem. The first time I tried it I thought there was no way I could come up with eight distinct solutions in only eight minutes, but I did. It's a great way to get your creative juices flowing. The process works well for jump-starting your design cycle and cross-pollinating ideas.

Now consider the even Crazier 8s of the standard work week. Come up with fresh design ideas for eight hours a day, five days a week. But generating ideas is the easy part. The concepts still must be researched, analyzed, compared, discarded, and iterated several times before the final solution reveals itself.

Sounds insane, right? Designers—your company's greatest potential resource for driving innovation—will hit a wall and burn out under these conditions. Designers needs time and distance between attempts at solutions before they can see them clearly.

Expecting a creative person to innovate eight hours per day (especially in a cube farm) is a ridiculous vestige of the industrial age. You can turn screws on

an assembly line for eight hours a day, but you can't mass produce innovations this way.

I used to tell my internal design team that one great design concept created in a thirty-minute lightning strike of inspiration is worth eight hours of grinding away at your desk. When inspiration refuses to show up, get up, go somewhere, and do something else. Often, it's during those uninspired hours in the week when your subconscious is working on the problem that the solution presents itself.

I gave my team this latitude with regards to time—not to circumvent my employer's policies—but to serve their best interests. The design concept that materializes in that 30-minute burst of insight can make the difference between leading and following in your industry, the difference between setting the product experience bar so high that no competitor can catch you versus languishing in a crowded field of mediocrity.

Conjuring design solutions out of the ether requires a deep understanding of the problem, of the people who have the problem, of the conditions under which people have the problem, of the root cause of the problem, and of the constraints surrounding the problem. All these dimensions need to ferment simultaneously in the designer's mind. But that's not all: you must mix in tangential ingredients—at your daughter's soccer game, while hiking in the mountains, by reading a book, or by watching a movie—before your multidimensional understanding of the problem can be distilled into a single solution. This requires time away from your desk. Employers must never misinterpret the office hiatus as time away from working on the problem.

Sometimes you must defy your company's policies to serve the company's best interests. As Gifford Pinchot III says in his *Intrepreneur's Ten Commandments*, this takes courage and the willingness to "Come into work each day willing to be fired."

https://intrapreneur.com/the-intrapreneurs-ten-commandments/

Place

Several years ago, I conducted a series of UX design workshops in locations throughout the USA and Europe. I promised participants that we would ask and answer a series of questions that would guide them to a multi-million-dollar solution to a hard design problem they were struggling with. It worked every time.

The hotel conference rooms that I sometimes rented for these events were sterile and windowless—hardly the sort of places that inspire innovative thinking.

By the time I got to Seattle, I was burned out. The workshops had become automatic, routine, and uninspired. I think the dreary rooms where I held them had finally drained the passion out of me.

So, without thinking about it too much, about one hour into the presentation I moved all the participants outside to the grounds of the hotel where we could see the sky, feel the breeze, smell the grass, and hear the birds. I wouldn't have the crutch of my PowerPoint slides, but I was more interested in connecting with the people in attendance and engaging them in conversation—not just clicking through another lecture. I wanted my participants to interact, share their stories, and work with me to arrive at that "Ah-ha!" moment.

I wanted them to be inspired. I needed to be inspired, too.

That spontaneous session produced several requests to deliver on-site versions of my workshop, including two with a major software company in the area. Thankfully, these company-sponsored events were conducted as offsites in inspirational venues surrounded by pine trees and waterfalls, rather than in featureless corporate conference rooms.

Your creative teams are charged with solving wicked-hard design problems. Yet to optimize the conditions under which these solutions are envisioned, tested, iterated, and designed, you confine them to work in a place for 40 hours per week that looks like this…?

Figure 18. A Place of Desperation

Is this a place that inspires innovation?

Or is this?

Figure 19. A Place of Inspiration

As leaders of creative teams, you need to care—not about how much time your team spends at their desks—but about giving them the latitude to go to places where inspiration—and therefore innovation—can flow. For some this may be a cabin in the mountains. For others an art museum. For others a sailboat on a lake. For others, their back-yard deck.

Places of inspiration are as diverse as the individuals on your team, and you should not expect them to think big thoughts in one-size-fits-all cube farms and sterile conference rooms. Giving your team the opportunity to work offsite is an investment in your company's future. It's not coddling your employees. It's not a boondoggle. You should care only about your team's results—not about where those results are achieved.

TRUST

Managers who exert control over their employee's time and place do so because they don't trust them to do their jobs unless they are closely monitored.

This paternalistic attitude that asserts employees require constant supervision is obsolete in the age of the knowledge worker. The mission of the manager of a creative team is to inspire, not to control. If results are accomplished and commitments are met, employees should have the agency to decide how, where, and when their work gets done.

The design problems that creatives must solve often require a weeks-long immersion to analyze the data, form clear problem statements, conjure up concepts, reject them, and start all over again. For weeks, there may be no tangible progress. But then the breakthrough comes—a concept that has the potential to transform the user experience and with it the company's fortunes. However, breakthroughs will never come if the creative team's manager doesn't trust the designer to persevere until the problem is solved.

This doesn't mean you ignore your employees for long periods of time. You should still practice MBWA—Managing By Walking Around—even if it's virtually. You still check in with your team regularly, not to monitor their work but to clear away barriers, empathize with their struggles, and celebrate their victories—and to express confidence in their imminent success. Do this, and you will motivate your talented designers to push through barriers and deliver great results.

Will you sometimes have slackers on your team? Sure. They slip through the cracks occasionally. I had one direct report who did absolutely nothing for several months, but eventually his AWOL was exposed and he resigned. But you should not make general policy based on the occasional disappointment. Trusting employees must be your default approach, even if you get burned sometimes.

ENERGY

Creativity cannot be timeboxed into forty-hour work weeks and confined to windowless office conference rooms. But there's an exception to these rules: give a creative team a hard problem to solve, put them in featureless room with whiteboards, projectors, Post-it® notes, Legos® (and whatever other toys you can think of) and watch the energy flow!

Creative teams thrive on challenges, and if you have the right mix of personalities and diversity of ideas, they can work together anywhere. "Together" is the operative word. If you have fostered a microculture in which everyone is respected, where no idea is a dumb idea, and in which the team genuinely enjoys working with each other—magic will happen in that room. One person's idea becomes the seed for the next person's idea. Designers furiously sketch concepts and fight (in a friendly way) over the dry erase marker. Time and place disappear, replaced by the dynamism of a team that collectively can solve any problem you throw at them.

Unfortunately, this creative energy cannot be simulated in a Zoom or MS Teams meeting. Even if you have a cohesive and mature team that has been working together for years, you can't fabricate the same level of vibrancy through a computer screen. Virtual team meetings work fine for discussions and presentations, but not for free-flowing design jams.

If you have a geographically distributed team, you need to get them together in the same place at least once a quarter, or whenever you are starting a new project that requires the expertise of the entire team to get it off the ground. If you have a large team and can't get everyone in the same place, form co-located sub teams to work on parts of the problem.

Work on the problem for a half-day or so or until the energy wanes. Frequent, intermittent bursts of ideation are better than long slogs. Ideas need to germinate, so allow at least a half day—and ideally a full day—for each member of the team to cogitate on the problem and work independently in a place and at a time of their choosing. When you assemble again, an entirely new slate of concepts and insights will have revealed themselves. For big design problems, set aside a conference room as a "war room" so that all the artifacts can be preserved from one session to the next.

While much of a designer's time is spent working independently to support the Agile development team, for big challenges requiring true innovation, nothing can replace the creative energy generated from assembling your team in the same place and turning them loose!

Failure

I once had the honor of leading (and being led by) a team that consistently produced outstanding designs that delighted both our customers and our leadership team…except one time. Our one failure involved designing a completely new experience for a cohort of users who had an extremely low tolerance for technology. The design solution would have to be both visually engaging and extraordinarily simple.

After several iterations, the "final" concept was shared with the organization in a design review. Afterwards, the CTO pulled me aside and as gently as possible told me that he and the rest of the leadership team were disappointed with our design.

It's never fun to hear that your stakeholders believe your team has failed. We were discouraged, but only for an hour or so.

I called an impromptu meeting with the team and shared the feedback with them. Yes, it's a cliché in business to recast every setback as an opportunity, but this one really was. I told the team (and believed it myself) that this failure was an opportunity to be heroes. No one—and especially not our competitors—had succeeded in designing a solution that satisfied the big unmet needs of this cohort of users. Our team was uniquely qualified to be the first. If we could put this temporary failure behind us and demonstrate to our stakeholders that we had the talent and the persistence to solve this problem, our eminence within the organization would skyrocket.

We had only a few days to deliver a new concept to the leadership team. While the mission before us was urgent, the challenge was also liberating. We abandoned all constraints and let our creative juices run wild. Of course, we didn't produce just one alternative design, but five unique solutions, each with a different theme. (To be clear, though, as director of the team, I issued the challenge and backed off, giving the designers the time and space they needed to ideate, design, and iterate. So, when I say "we," I really mean "they." The designers deserve all the credit.)

The new designs were a huge success and confidence in our team was restored. In just a matter of days, we had turned what could have been a debilitating failure into a resounding success.

Professor Rosabeth Moss Kanter once said that "in the middle, everything looks like a failure." Everyone fails sometimes, but failure is only temporary if we have the persistence and confidence to push past it, to learn from it, and to see it as an opportunity for even greater success. As the leader of a creative team, you do this by reframing the failure as a challenge and expressing confidence that your team is uniquely qualified to conquer it.

PERFORMANCE

Because I have managed creative teams for over thirty years, there have been over thirty times in my career when I seriously considered quitting my job.

The potentially job-terminating event begins with a meeting of all managers in the division. In preparation for the meeting, each manager has rank-ordered and assigned a number to each member of their team based on their "performance" over the past year, ranging from a "5" for outstanding performance to a "1" for unsatisfactory performance.

A bloody battle ensues in which the contributions of marketers are compared to call center agents, technical writers are ranked against software engineers, and UX designers are evaluated against product managers. To ensure conflict, each performance category has a "target" percentage assigned to it: 15% for 5s and 4s, 15% for 2s and 1s, and 70% for the middling 3s.

Managers come armed with evidence of the stellar results their superstars have produced and hide in their back pockets a list of employees who may need to be sacrificed to meet the category quotas. Top performers from the previous year tend to stay at the top, but sometimes, after metaphorically comparing Marie Curie, Albert Einstein, Isaac Newton, and Harriet Tubman as candidates for the 5s, Einstein is demoted to a 4 to meet the target percentages. Moving up requires extraordinary achievement, although the precise qualifications for "exceeding expectations" are a mystery. Most of the time upward mobility is based on which employees are "visible" to the most managers.

Over the course of the following week, the manager summons each employee to a conference room to disclose which number the entirety of their past year's work has been reduced to. The employee has completed a self-evaluation beforehand describing their results across a dozen or so performance criteria, and the manager searches for ways to restate the employee's assessment in different words. Sometimes the manager is *required* to include "opportunities for growth" (i.e., negative comments) in the feedback to balance out the praise for accomplishments.

Maybe you've had this experience; I hope that you haven't. In many of my management jobs across multiple companies, this is the way performance reviews worked. It's hard to imagine a better way to demotivate employees at the start of a new fiscal year.

But it doesn't have to be this way. You could, for example, give every member of your team a 5 rating (I did). If your boss or HR won't let you get away with that, you can explain that company "policy" requires you to assign each person a number but that the numbers are meaningless and don't reflect your true assessment of their contribution.

Instead of calling your employees into a conference room to deliver the performance review, you could take them out to lunch. And instead of rehashing their past performance (including the requisite negative "development opportunities"), you could talk about the future. Discuss the challenges and opportunities your department will face in the coming year. Talk about their career goals and brainstorm how to align them to the company's objectives. Ask what career opportunities you can provide to support their interests. Express your confidence in their ability to make the upcoming year their best year ever. And always end the meeting by thanking them for all that they've done and all that they are about to do.

Tell them, "You've done great work this past year...but it's not your best work. Your best work will be on your next project. Your best work is ahead of you."

(Imagine how sad it would be to think that your best work is behind you.)

Violating HR policies for performance reviews may be politically dangerous, but it may be the most important thing you can do to retain valuable employees and help your company prosper. An inspired employee produces better results than a demotivated one.

Isn't that in the company's best interests?

Hiring

Getting approval for a job requisition is an exciting and dangerous time. Exciting because you have an opportunity to strengthen your UX team with additional expertise and diversity. Dangerous because hiring the wrong person will disrupt team dynamics and damage esprit de corps.

Whether the new hire has stellar UX skills is not the worry. Training and mentoring can address deficiencies in tool proficiency or design chops. What you can't remedy in a new hire is a deficit of empathy, humility, honesty, and emotional intelligence.

I've made the mistake of hiring designers with outstanding portfolios who lacked these soft skills. Unlike developers and contractors who can work in isolation from others, UXers must be natural collaborators. Otherwise, the effort you've invested to cultivate relationships with the other departments will be destroyed by the attitudes and actions of one supercilious designer.

How do you detect whether the job candidate sitting in front of you has the personal qualities you are looking for? You'll usually know within the first five minutes of the interview.

As they tell their story, ask yourself the following questions:

- Do they have a passion for solving problems?

- Are they self-deprecating and do they have a good sense of humor?

- Can they walk you through their portfolio and tell stories about the projects they've worked on?

- How do they react to constructive criticism?

- Do they take all the credit for themselves, or do they share it with their colleagues?

- Can they describe career failures and what they learned from them?

Ask members of the UX team to interview the candidates, as well as one product manager, one product owner, and one developer. If your colleagues are uncertain whether they can work well with the person, you should consider other candidates.

One final bit of advice: *don't* base your hiring decision on a design test! The candidate probably already has a job that consumes her time and creative energy during her most productive hours. Whatever creative neurons are left over at the end of the day will be applied to the design test.

She will not have time to iterate. She will not understand your product domain. She will not be familiar with your design system, product roadmap, or future vision. She will not have the benefit of user research.

Design tests are incredibly stressful. Nobody does their best work under such overwhelming pressure. Rely upon it to choose your next hire, and you may pass on your next superstar. Instead, look at the prospective employee's body of work and ask them to tell you about the stories behind it.

Esprit de Corps

Esprit de corps—a French term that Oxford Languages defines as "a feeling of pride, fellowship, and common loyalty shared by members of a particular group"—is essential to your UX team's success. This degree of comradery is not something you can manufacture, but you can establish a microculture that nurtures it.

Nothing brings a UX team together like challenging them to collaborate on solving a big design problem. We called these team projects design jams.

Following Steve Blank's GOOB advice, we'd **G**et **O**ut **O**f the **B**uilding to an informal setting conducive to inspiration. We'd go to a hotel on a beach, or to a cabin in the mountains, or sometimes just to a coffee shop.

We'd spend three days working on the problem: a half day on the first day, the entire next day, and a half day on the final day, with breaks in between for individual work. We sketch, we'd debate, we'd invent, we'd discard. No one person ran the show. If you had an idea you wanted to share, the current leader would toss you a plush toy frog. Whomever had the frog led that portion of the jam while everyone else listened.

Field trips also build team cohesion. Once when starting a gamification project, our team traveled to the office of the foremost expert in the field to help us plan our approach. And because inspiration can strike anywhere, we'd schedule recreational outings to Top Golf and escape rooms. One member of our team hosted us on his boat on a hot summer afternoon; another had us over for a pig roast. Over the holidays, I invited the team to my house to talk about plans for the new year while I cooked lunch for them.

If you succeed at esprit de corps, your team's default modus operandi will always be collaboration rather than competition. They will value their colleagues' special talents and perspectives and ask them for help and advice. They will never stop challenging and debating each other, but will always do so with respect, curiosity, and an open mind.

Your company may have outdated command and control policies that undermine your attempts to establish esprit de corps. It may have performance programs that foster competition among employees or workloads that make it difficult to carve out time for field trips and design jams.

Don't let that stop you. Diligently and methodically construct your UX microculture despite the rules imposed by the larger corporate culture. Work underground if you must. Your company executives may not comprehend it, but by nurturing a culture where your creatives can thrive, you are fulfilling your mission as a UX leader.

Part 4. Selling UX

UX design is better understood now than it was ten years ago, but it remains an esoteric concept to most. Design hardware? People get that. Ditto with software & website UIs. But designing an "experience?" How do you do that?

Early in my career, I tried without success to evangelize the value of UX to others in my company. I made presentations describing the UCD process and provided my colleagues with a menu of services that the UX team offered the organization. No change in UX maturity resulted.

I tried engaging the leaders in the company with design thinking sessions. The results were better, but the products didn't improve. The workshop was fun and informative, but after it was over, everyone went back to their "real" jobs.

I once taught a mandatory four-hour UX course. Everyone in the division was required to attend. The course was highly rated, but in the short span of four hours, there was no time to actually *do* UX, so participants left with some appreciation of the field but failed to understand their part in it.

It took me several years to realize that selling UX to an organization is a process, not a presentation. My most successful attempt was a two-day workshop in which we applied the mindsets, models, and methods of UX on actual projects. Each participant came to the class with a real design problem they were struggling with, and by the end of the workshop, they had solved it. But even this was a one-off success; it didn't change the culture.

As described in Part 1, you can sell UX to individuals and groups by understanding their drivers and collaborating with them on win-win projects. But to sell UX to the leadership team and change the corporate culture, you will need more than passionate arguments and incremental improvements. You'll need business justifications. You'll need data. And to demonstrate the transformative potential of UX investment, you'll need a breakthrough project.

The Wizard of Oz Syndrome

If you seek approval for an innovative UX initiative from your boss, you will likely run head-on into the Wizard of Oz Syndrome.

Remember that managers and executives are fiscally accountable to investors and are reluctant to fund a project without the high probability of a positive ROI. Just doing the "right thing" for the customer is not a sufficient argument.

In the *Wizard of Oz*, Dorothy asks the wizard to take her and her dog Toto back to Kansas. The wizard agrees, but only after Dorothy brings him the broom from the Wicked Witch of the West.

In business, the same technique is used to delay or defeat UX initiatives while simultaneously appearing to support them. The conversation goes something like this:

You: "Hey boss, I have a great idea for an innovative solution to a customer pain point."

Boss: "Great! Show me the ROI data for your idea."

You: "I don't have ROI data. But I'm sure this would dramatically improve our customer experience."

Boss: "No data? Bring me the data and then we'll talk."

The demand for ROI data is used as a stop sign for innovative but potentially expensive ideas. It's an executive's way of avoiding risk while seeming to applaud your creative initiative.

There are two ways to respond to the Wizard of Oz challenge:

- Bring back the broom (i.e., the data), or

- Work underground to gather research evidence and create a prototype, then recruit colleagues to your cause.

This part of the book provides strategies for both.

My Story: Two Postcards from Oz

Earlier I told the story of how I transitioned from documenting complexity to designing simplicity with the invention of the intelligent *PIG* (see *Cultivating Relationships with Documentation*).

After I built a prototype of the knowledge-based system and developed a story demonstrating how the peripheral installation experience could be dramatically simplified, I solicited my boss' help in moving the project forward.

He sat down with me at my desk. I pulled out the *PIG* manual and walked him through the written instructions for installing a printer on a UNIX workstation, a process that required, among other difficult things, typing and executing this UNIX command:

```
nohup sleep 2000000000 < /dev/lp3186 & sty —parenb
-ienqak cs8 9600 —cstopb —clocal ixon opost onlcr
tab3 < /dev/lp3186
```

Then I showed him my intelligent *PIG* prototype and the much simpler experience it delivered. I thought he would be impressed, but he frowned through the entire demonstration. When it was over, he said:

"Good job, John. Interesting idea."

Then he got up and went back to his desk. Not another word about the proposal was spoken. I'm sure he was thinking (but didn't say), "Your job is to write manuals, not design software. Just do you job."

There was not even an offer to come back to him with ROI data; the idea was dead on arrival. The wizard would not even contemplate taking me back to Kansas.

A few years later, in the days before laptops, I hauled my tower computer and monitor from Colorado to California to meet with the vice president of my division. I was there to request funding for a revolutionary initiative that would have secured the company's reputation as the ease-of-use leader in its market. At this point in my career, I was a passionate idealist, not a businessman, and I neglected to bring along the spreadsheets and pie charts showing the return on investment.

I set up my computer in a conference room and walked him through my demonstration. When I was done, he told me I showed "good initiative."

He sent me on my way, assuring me the funds for the project would be granted when I came back with a cost/benefit analysis proving that the company's money would be well spent. I was still naïve enough to believe that doing the right thing for the customer—reducing pain points and fulfilling big unmet needs—would be self-justifying, requiring no further proof of potential success.

I was yet another casualty of the Wizard of Oz Syndrome, but unlike Dorothy, I had no idea how to retrieve the witch's broom (i.e., how to collect ROI data to make the business case for UX). I never completed my quest back then, but since that time I've discovered a few remedies to the Wizard of Oz Syndrome that I'll share in the following sections.

The Breakthrough Project

Simplicity is the ultimate disruptive innovation. If your simplicity initiative succeeds, accolades will pour in from customers, from sales, from marketing, from support, and from the executive leadership team. As the catalyst for the innovation, you will be lauded as a hero, a visionary, the corporation's MVP. This is great for your career if you do it right; it's disastrous if you do it wrong.

To drive cultural change in an organization that doesn't yet appreciate UX, you must go big. You must find a big unmet need or costly pain point, identify its root cause, and solve for it. Incremental improvements are not going to cut it. You must conceive and execute a breakthrough project.

You will find the big unmet need or costly pain point through user research. Get out into the field and observe users where they work or conduct virtual observations over video conference if you can't visit them in person. Get customers on the record with voice or video recordings describing their goals and frustrations.

Once you've identified the problem, you need to build a compelling, medium-fidelity prototype of your solution that stands in stark contrast to the experience your product delivers today. Your prototype must be interactive, and it must tell a story. It must have sufficient polish to get the attention of colleagues who are impressed by "cool" designs, but not so polished that it looks ready to ship. Leave some gaps in your solution (some problems left unsolved); you'll need them later when you expand the project team.

In this early phase of the breakthrough project, you are working underground. If you announce to your colleagues (and even worse, to the executive leadership team) that you have an idea for a breakthrough project, the corporate immune system will rise up to defeat you. NIH—Not Invented Here—Syndrome is very real, and colleagues will summarily dismiss your idea because they were offered no part in shaping it.

Work by yourself or with other members of the UX team to refine the prototype before exposing it to the wider organization. The purpose of the early prototype is to generate excitement for its game-changing potential, and—most importantly—to enlist the help of the Four-Legged Stool in refining it.

At the end of this phase, you should have three pieces of ammunition in your arsenal:

- Research videos showing customers struggling with your product's pain points, articulating their big unmet needs, and describing how they wished your product would work.

- A medium-fidelity prototype of your proposed breakthrough solution.

- Before and after UX analysis proving how your proposed prototype is vastly superior to your current product's experience.

Next, schedule an informal meeting with the product manager and present your three pieces of ammunition. Close the meeting by asking for their help in conducting more research, iterating the prototype, solving problems you still need to solve, and co-presenting the initiative to the rest of the organization.

Once the product manager is on board, schedule a meeting with you, the product manager, the lead developer, and product owner to consider your proposal. Respond to any objections or skepticism with:

"See, that's why I need your help. Our customers are telling us this is a very real unmet need. You raise valid questions. I value your insights, and I'd like us to work together to see where we go from here. Maybe it goes nowhere, but let's give it a shot."

If you time this right and propose the idea with the right amount of humility, you will disarm the corporate immune system and move the project forward.

After several working sessions with the Four-Legged Stool, you will be ready to pitch the breakthrough initiative to the next level of leadership. Together with your core team, ask for your boss' help in tightening up the business case and formulating answers to the ELT's likely questions and concerns.

Armed with the voice of the customer, a polished prototype, a compelling business case, and at least one high-level sponsor, you and the core team are ready to jointly propose the project to the ELT. If you have chosen your problem wisely and visualized a breakthrough solution, there's a good chance your project will generate excitement and move forward.

After the project is funded and scheduled, execute as you would any other project with continuous research, discovery, and refinement. Provide your prototype to sales as a release preview to close deals and gather additional feedback prior to release. After release, track the metrics that matter: new account wins attributable to the project, revenue generated through renewals, and cost reductions in support calls and product returns.

By the time your breakthrough project ships, you will have rallied the support of the entire organization, proven its impact on financial metrics, and shared the credit with your core partners. This is how you pilot your company toward a UX-driven culture.

Now all you have to do is…do it again.

The Business Case for UX

Someday launching a project to repair a broken customer experience won't require a herculean justification; it will be one of those "just do it" initiatives whose business benefits are accepted on principle. A meeting will be called. The issue will be raised. A solution will be proposed. All heads will nod in unison. The go-ahead will be given on the conviction that fixing the product now will be cheaper than rebuilding the customer base later.

Someday this will be the way things work, but in your company's current culture, today may not be that day. You may work in a world in which a customer-serving initiative cannot be undertaken without a thorough ROI analysis, a half-dozen market research studies, a few usability tests, and a management "sponsor" who is willing to accept the risk of financing the project. No wonder so many innovators die of exhaustion! If Thomas Edison had worked for a modern risk-averse company, we'd still be illuminating our homes by gaslight.

So be it. To win this war, you will need to meet your leadership team on its own terms, armed with an arsenal of irrefutable research data and incontrovertible logic.

But first a word about customer loyalty versus satisfaction.

Loyalty versus Satisfaction

Before launching into the business reasons for investing in UX, you will need to connect the dots between customer loyalty/satisfaction and a world-class user experience.

Customer loyalty is often measured by customer responses to an NPS (Net Promoter Score) questionnaire. On a scale of 1-10, current customers may be asked:

- How would you rate your satisfaction with our product?

- Would you buy another product from our company?

- Would you recommend this product to others?

If a customer gives high scores to each question—meaning the customer loves the product, would buy another product from the company without hesitation, and is telling everyone she knows how great the product is—then the customer is deemed loyal to the brand.

A *satisfied* customer is different from a *loyal* customer. A satisfied customer is lukewarm about her experience with your product. She will answer the three loyalty questions somewhere in the middle of the scale. A satisfied customer thinks the product does what she expects it to do, but it does not exceed her expectations. She might buy from this company again but she might not, depending on factors like price and availability. Or she might just feel like trying another brand.

Research has shown that satisfied customers are a fickle lot at best. Harvard Business Review, for example, reported that 65-85% of customers who were merely *satisfied* with their last purchase switched brands without hesitation.

Customer acquisition costs—the money your company spends to convert a potential customer into an actual customer—can wipe out much of the profit on a customer's first purchase. Repeat purchases are needed before significant profit is earned, but second and third purchases will not be awarded unless the customer is *highly* satisfied with her first purchase. For example, one printer company found that customers scoring a 9 or 10 on a 10-point customer satisfaction scale would purchase 2.5 times as many printers in next 12 months than those giving scores from 0-8.

Loyal customers are profitable, so how does a company inspire loyalty? It's easier to understand what *prevents* a customer from becoming loyal.

If I buy a new toaster that burns my first piece of toast, I am frustrated. If it burns my second piece of toast, I may get angry. If it burns every third piece of toast for the next year, I won't be loyal. I'm not even satisfied. I may even become a "product assassin" who will advise everyone I know to avoid buying that brand.

If I buy a new toaster and it toasts my first piece of bread perfectly, I am delighted. If it continues to work perfectly and effortlessly, I will become loyal. When it comes to toasters, I've found my brand for life.

Now the connection between loyalty and user experience. Customer loyalty is determined by the customer's experience with the product, which is in turn determined by product's design and behavior. Therefore, if you want loyal customers, you must design a product that gives customers *what* they want (e.g., toast), the *way* they want it (browned but not burned), with as little effort and hassle as possible.

Duh, right? Then why do so many companies fail to reach this basic conclusion? Because logic fails them; they want data instead.

So, as you peruse the following reasons for investing in UX, remember that a customer's loyalty is primarily determined by how easily the product delivers the results your brand promised them.

Now we have arrived at the fundamental data-collection questions:

- How does a great UX increase revenue?

- How does a great UX reduce costs?

- And how will a poor UX decrease revenue and increase costs?

Note: The following justifications cite statistics from several studies. By themselves, these stats are useless. To use them effectively, you must apply them to your business financials and calculate how these stats would affect your own revenues, costs, and market share.

The Scenario

You have uncovered a particularly egregious instance of user abuse and have designed a UX solution to fix it. Unfortunately, your colleagues don't share your enthusiasm. They barrage your proposal with the usual objections:

We can't slip the schedule.

We don't have the resources.

It's not a priority for this release.

The challenge before you is clear: you must prove to your colleagues that redesigning the user experience is not just the *nice* thing to do—it is the *profitable* thing to do.

The following business justifications may help you articulate your arguments. Not all will apply to your business, but those that do may help convince your colleagues and leadership team to look beyond the short-term costs of UX redesign to the long-term savings and revenue potential of these efforts.

Do *not* build a PowerPoint deck, get on your soapbox, and preach these justifications to your colleagues and leaders. Instead, apply them to your financials and work them into discussions, along with supporting evidence you have uncovered through user research. Come prepared with a prototype of your proposed solution, and a simplicity scorecard that proves how your redesign removes a big pain point in the current user experience.

Justification 1: Your Company Cannot Succeed Unless Your Customers Do

> Rationale:
>
> - Your company wants to increase revenue and reduce costs.
>
> - Your company generates more revenue when your customers succeed; your company accrues more costs when your customers fail.
>
> - Customers measure success by how easily they can achieve promised results with your products.
>
> - Therefore, for your company to increase revenues and reduce costs, your customers must succeed.

Aside from the airline executive who once remarked, "As long as they're born faster than we can make them hate us, we're in business," most companies think it's a good idea to retain their current customers. The only sure way to retain customers is to know what they want and help them succeed in getting it.

What do customers want? I've said it before: **results.**

Customers buy products to help them achieve results. When a customer buys a tax preparation product, she expects it to help her complete her tax returns. When a customer buys a bread machine, he expects it to help him make the perfect loaf of bread. Tax returns and bread loaves are results. The product must deliver these results—no excuses—or the customer will fail and so will the product and so will the company.

Any competent company can design a product *capable* of producing results. ENIAC was capable of producing results, provided it had very smart and highly-trained people to operate it. So why do so many customers struggle to get results with the products they buy? Because there is another much higher standard by which customers measure success.

It's called **experience**.

Companies fail when the experience of achieving results with their products demands more effort from their customers than they are willing to tolerate. If the tax preparation software requires the customer to understand a lot of accounting terminology and government regulations, she will abandon the software and let her accountant prepare her returns instead. If the bread machine doesn't work well at high altitudes, the customer will return the machine to the store and buy his bread from the bakery.

Despite each product's *capabilities*, its customers—and thus the company—failed because the *experience* was found wanting.

If the product demands too much from its customers, they will decide the effort of use outweighs its potential benefits—despite its lightning-fast performance and impressive feature set.

Your company may think your user experience is just fine as is. But if…

- you have high customer turnover and low customer loyalty, or

- your products are getting flamed on the internet, or

- you provide a large documentation set for your product or require customers to attend product training, or

- you receive lots of support calls or hits on your support website, or

- your products are returned with no trouble found, then…

…your user experience is costing your company money. According to Lee Resources, there's a 91% chance that customers who had a negative experience with your product won't do business with you again.

To increase revenue and reduce costs, your company must design the user experience as carefully as it designs product functionality. It must recognize that even the most powerful product is useless if customers can't easily achieve results with it. It must design out the demands the product foists upon its customers, one by one, until results come effortlessly.

Why? Because your company cannot succeed unless your customers do.

How to Sell It

Step 1

Work with your finance, product management, or sales department to gather sales data over the past year. Ask for a breakdown of revenue from new customers versus revenue from repeat/renewal customers. If your company gathers data on the reasons for lost sales and renewals, identify causes attributable to a poor user experience and calculate their costs.

Step 2

Identify the most cumbersome experience in your product. If you have several candidates, pick one. Conduct user research and record customers expressing their frustration.

Next, prototype multiple solutions, one that is a simple fix (perhaps a change in navigation or labeling), one that requires moderate development effort, and one that is best but more time consuming and expensive to implement.

Step 3

During release planning, make your pitch to correct the UX problem to your partners, tying the revenue data to the poor experience and demonstrating how your prototype would improve the experience (and thus improve revenue).

Ask these questions:

- If we maintain the status quo, will our current customers buy from us again or defect to a competitor who provides a better experience?

- If we redesign this feature, will we attract and retain more customers?

These are rhetorical questions, but its more effective to make your colleagues think about the questions rather than feed them the answers.

Justification 2: The Power of One

Rationale:

- Your company wants to increase revenue by increasing the size of its customer base.

- *Prospective* customers will decide which product to buy based on *current* customers' ratings and reviews.

- Ratings and reviews are based upon *current* customers' experience with your product.

- More prospective customers will choose your product when they see mostly positive reviews.

- Fewer prospective customers will choose your product when they see mostly negative reviews.

- Therefore, to increase your customer base, your company must encourage current customers to write positive reviews by delivering a delightful user experience.

In the age of social media, the voice of the customer has a megaphone. Online product review sites afford *current* customers the power to positively or negatively influence the purchasing decisions of thousands of *potential* customers. Both loyal and dissatisfied customers are stepping up to the megaphone. Which voice speaks loudest is up to you.

When you amaze your customers with an outstanding experience, they will tell everyone they know—and even everyone they don't know—how awesome your product is. These testimonials are far more credible and persuasive than any advertising campaign your company could devise.

Elegant product behavior inspires unsolicited positive reviews, which generate new sales, which increase your customer base, which add to your revenue stream, which increase your profit—all without adding a penny to your marketing costs.

How much is one raving fan worth? She's worth much more than the purchase price of the product and much more than the repeat business she will award you in the future. This one raving fan could be worth thousands of dollars in referral sales.

The Power of One can create or it can destroy. Users who have a negative experience are 2-3 times more likely to write a review than users who have a positive experience. And it takes 40 positive reviews to undo the damage of 1 negative review.

Packrat, by Polaris Software, was the leading Personal Information Manager (PIM) software in the early 1990s. It enjoyed a market share of 27%—until the company released version 5.0 in 1993. The new product was feature-rich, powerful, and infinitely configurable. It was also buggy, often crashed, and had a cumbersome user interface. Fans of previous versions were furious and mercilessly flamed the new version on the company-sponsored online user forum. The mutiny spread, and by the time Polaris was able to release an update, its market share had plummeted to less than 10%. The damage to the company's reputation was irreparable. A few, very angry, very dedicated customer assassins were responsible for generating the anti-product fervor that brought the company down.

Malcom Gladwell made the Power of One abundantly clear in *The Tipping Point* with "The Law of the Few," which asserts that only a small number of people are required to start social epidemics. Mavens, Connectors, and Salespeople—people who influence others and disseminate ideas—have profound effects on the spread of information and attitudes. If you can please a Maven, you will recruit a powerful ally—perhaps the most potent salesperson on your "staff." Treat a Maven badly, and you create a brand assassin, dedicated to disrupting your sales and running your company into the ground.

How to Sell It

Step 1

Go to a website or other public forum where customers express their opinions and ratings. Google, Amazon, and virtually all sales channels now include reviews.

Calculate the ratio of positive reviews to negative reviews.

Capture the most positive and most scathing reviews. For each one, ask:

- Is this a loyal customer, a satisfied customer, or a dissatisfied customer?

- What did this customer like or dislike about our product?

- If a potential customer read this, would she purchase our product or look for another brand?

- What did we do right to warrant this positive review? Is there anything we could have done differently to prevent this negative review?

Step 2

Work with product management and finance to calculate hypothetical revenue costs:

- If a negative review dissuades just 1% of the market from purchasing our product, how much potential revenue would our company lose?

- If just 1% of your current customers have this negative experience— and studies indicate 91% of them won't do business with us again— how much renewal revenue will our company lose?

Justification 3: Reducing Support and Warranty Costs

Rationale:

- Your company wants to reduce the costs of technical support and NTF warranty returns.

- Users call support or return products when they can't achieve promised results.

- Therefore, you can reduce the costs of support and NTF returns by designing products that make it easy for users to achieve promised results.

A Quality Review article entitled "Don't Fix the Product, Fix the Customer" back in 1988 declared that two of every three support complaints were due to user misunderstandings, not product defects. Let's hope we are more enlightened today and recognize that a "user misunderstanding" *is* a product defect—a defect in the user experience.

Customers no longer have patience for products that don't work right away. I'm one of them. I once returned three different brands of video capture products to Best Buy in a single day. I couldn't get them to work right out of the box, so I returned them. The fourth product I purchased worked and I kept it.

When returned to the manufacturer, those first three video capture products would have been tested and classified as No Trouble Found (NTF) warranty returns. From the company's perspective, they had nothing wrong with them.

But of course, there *was* something wrong with them. The effort required to achieve the result I sought exceeded my tolerance. I did not have the patience to read the manuals, call support, and master the technology; I just wanted a simple product that delivered results within the first few minutes of use.

A returned product is the most expensive interaction your business can have with a customer. Your company incurs the costs of shipping, refurbishing, repackaging, and discounting the product for resale. Returns reduce revenue and generate negative reviews that may dissuade prospective customers from trusting your brand.

The root cause of these costs is a poor user experience. Despite your best efforts to educate customers through manuals, help systems, webinars, chatbots, online knowledge bases, video tutorials, and other "self-support" options, many will choose a support call as the most expedient solution. Others, like me, will not bother to call at all, but instead will opt to return the product to the store "with nothing wrong with it."

The only way to reduce support calls and NTF returns is to eliminate the demanding product behaviors that generate them.

How to Sell It

Step 1

Work with your support partners to identify all calls classified as user misunderstandings. Choose one of the most frequent calls and create a prototype to simplify the offending feature's experience.

Step 2

Count the NTF returns from the previous year. What was the specific product behavior that caused each product to be returned? If you're not sure, ask the sales team or retailers what customers are telling them when they return the product. If the product was returned shortly after purchase, you can hypothesize that the frustration occurred during installation and configuration.

Step 3

Once you have counts of support calls and NTF returns, multiply these numbers by the average cost of a support call or NTF return.

Compare the costs of treating the symptom of the UX problem—i.e., via support and warrant costs—to the cost of fixing the root cause of the problem—i.e., development resources and time to redesign the experience. Which is less expensive: fixing it once or incurring these costs year after year?

Step 4

If you're going to incur the costs of some support calls anyway, you can at least turn the cost of these calls into a strategy for retaining unhappy customers and avoiding the cost of recruiting new ones.

Some businesses refuse to take even the smallest steps to keep an existing customer. They hide behind policies: "I'm sorry, but our policy is XYZ and if we made an exception for you, we'd have to make an exception for everybody." Others stick to contracts: "I realize your warranty only expired four hours ago, but I'm afraid you'll just have to pay for a new product" (yes, but not from you!).

What would be the effect of empowering a service desk employee to wink at the customer and say, "I'm not supposed to do this, but for you I'll make an exception." Or giving a tech support agent the latitude to tell an irate customer, "You've had a rough day. I'm going to send you a $25 gift card and I hope you'll accept our sincere apologies for the aggravation we've caused you."

Customers who receive this kind of treatment are going to sit down and write you a glowing review. By showing some empathy and flexibility, you've created a customer for life and a pro bono sales rep. Sure it costs money to give a little in the short term, but it pays big in the long run.

Justification 4: The Silent Exodus

Rationale:

- Your company wants repeat customers.

- While excellent customer support can salvage a vulnerable customer relationship, the most at-risk customers will never contact support.

- 62% to 84% of customers who have a negative product experience and *do not* contact support will never buy from your company again.

- Therefore, because support cannot salvage a customer relationship if the customer doesn't call, the primary way to preserve repeat revenue is to eliminate known pain points in the user experience.

Staffing a call center to answer routine "How do I...?" questions is costly, but what is the cost when frustrated customers *don't* call technical support? You could be hemorrhaging customers at an alarming rate and not even know it.

Angry customers who contact technical support are clearly dissatisfied. They've encountered problems with your product and are calling to demand a solution or some other form of consideration. They are giving you one last opportunity to take the actions necessary to keep them as customers. If they receive a satisfactory resolution, 91% say they will consider buying from your company again.

Unfortunately, a Technical Assistance Research Programs (TARP) study found that for every four customers who complain, another *ninety-six* dissatisfied customers will never bother to contact you. And of those ninety-six, at least sixty-two—and as many as eighty-four—will never buy from you again. Instead, they will just silently walk away.

Now the good news. A study published in the Harvard Business Review found that increasing your customer retention rate by just 5% can grow your company's profits by at least 25%, and perhaps as much as 85%.

How can you significantly increase your retention rate? By never giving your customers a reason to leave. How? By delivering an outstanding user experience. A great product experience will impress 100% of your customers, but great support experience will only influence the 4% who bother to call.

Your product is your only guaranteed point of contact with your customers—you must make it count. To avoid the lost revenue and customer replacement costs caused by silent defections, you must design a product that surprises and delights your customers and inspires loyalty—a product that "just works."

How to Sell It

Step 1

- Count a year's worth of angry customer support calls about a high-frequency UX issue.

- Divide this number by 0.04 to calculate the *total* number of dissatisfied customers, including those that did not bother to contact you.

- Now multiply this number by .96 to calculate the number of dissatisfied, *non-complaining* customers.

- Multiply this number by 0.65. This is the minimum number of non-complaining customers you lost according to the TARP study.

- Multiply the dissatisfied, non-complaining customers by 0.90. This is the maximum number of customers you may have lost.

These numbers may seem unrealistic and can vary widely depending on the type of products you sell. But the point is this: many customers who feel wronged by your product will silently abandon your brand and never give you the opportunity to win them back. If the number of customer defections is only 10% of the number you calculated, it is still a large number. And when you combine this with the costs of acquiring a new replacement customer, the impact on your bottom line can be substantial.

Step 2

Next:

- Build one or more prototypes that demonstrate how the user experience can be redesigned to eliminate the issue.

- Estimate the development cost of implementing the redesign and compare it to the cost of losing customers who quietly defect because of this issue.

- The cost of fixing the issue is probably much less than the cost of doing nothing.

- Implement the fix.

- Three months after the redesigned product is released, verify that calls on this UX issue have dramatically declined. Publicize your results.

Justification 5: Lost Employee Productivity

> Rationale:
>
> - Your company wants to achieve the highest possible productivity from its labor costs.
>
> - Complex IT applications and cumbersome business processes reduce employee productivity.
>
> - Therefore, to maximize labor ROI, increase productivity by simplifying complex IT applications and business processes.

I once overheard a group of people in the cafeteria laughing about how they had spent their morning. One of them had inadvertently clicked something in Microsoft Word that caused paragraph marks to appear everywhere. She didn't want to see paragraph marks, and after several attempts to turn them off, she asked one of her coworkers for help. A few minutes later, they recruited another coworker, then another, until there were four people working on the problem. An hour later, they succeeded in turning off the paragraph marks. (To Microsoft's credit, they have since made it easier to turn "formatting marks" on and off.)

This story is an example of the "futz factor" in action—the time office workers spend "futzing" around with technology, trying to get it to work. Sausalito-based SBT Accounting Systems surveyed 6,000 users and found the average office worker spent 5.1 hours per week trying to solve mundane problems with their computers. Multiply this by the number of employees and the cost of lost productivity is significant.

If you design applications that run the internal operations of your company, simplifying the UX is just as important as it is for customer-facing apps. Poorly designed applications are a time sink. Factor in the time spent by help desk staff to assist confused users, and this lost productivity can cost the company tens of thousands of dollars per year or more.

How to Sell It

Step 1

To make the business case for more investment in the UX of internal applications, start by shadowing your help desk technicians. Find out which applications receive the most calls for help and how long it takes them to resolve each issue. Ask the callers how long they have been "futzing" with the problem before calling the help desk.

Step 2

Next, perform a thorough UX analysis of the troublesome application. Capture all the actions the user must complete to achieve desired results. Analyze the findability of the information they must know to complete each action.

Create one or more prototypes that streamline the workflow and eliminate the pain points you found.

Step 3

Estimate how many employees use the application and how frequently they use it. (Use the volume of helpdesk calls as an indicator but remember that most people will just futz with the problem until they resolve it.) Finally, estimate the lost productivity time and the financial cost of that lost time.

Here's how I used steps 1-3 when I once led a large team of UX designers that supported the company's IT applications ....

Our team was responsible for designing nearly one hundred applications that supported all aspects of the company's business operations. One of the company's most complex applications was a conference room scheduling program.

To demonstrate the costs of this application in lost employee productivity, I wrote a typical user story—"Reserve a conference room for 12 people from 1-2pm on August 4th"—and created a storyboard with screenshots of every interaction a user would experience while trying to achieve this result. I then quantified the primary UX metrics for the story:

- The number of screens navigated: 9

- The number of user actions (e.g., clicks): 54

- The number of duplicate entries (i.e., the number of times a user had to reenter data that she had previously entered): 11

- The number of moments of truth, pain points, and moments of confusion: 33

I worked with my UX team to design an interactive prototype of a new and improved application and captured the same metrics:

- The number of screens navigated: 3, down from 9

- The number of user actions (e.g., clicks): 3, down from 54

- The number of duplicate entries: 0, down from 11

- The number of moments of truth, pain points, and moments of confusion: 0, down from 33

I then estimated the cost savings the company could expect from improved employee productivity:

- 10,000 users per month...

- Multiplied by 5 room reservations per user per month...

- Multiplied by 4 minutes saved per room reservation (a conservative estimate)...

- Multiplied by the average per-minute salary of an employee—$0.70...

- Equals 3,333 hours and $140,000 saved per month.

I thought this was a very convincing business case for redesigning the application. However, due to the large volume of projects we supported each year, I could not recruit a sponsor and the redesign never rose to the top in priority.

Epilogue: My Biggest Political Mistake

Due to a political miscalculation, the greatest success of my career was nearly my greatest failure.

I followed all the steps described in this book. I conducted a listening tour. I observed customers and recorded their frustrations and suggestions. I identified a big unmet need and launched a breakthrough project.

Working underground to avoid triggering the corporate immune system, I envisioned a new design paradigm that profoundly improved the user experience. I hired a contractor—a true UX genius with whom I had worked before—to help me develop a cool, interactive prototype. I performed a compelling before-and-after experience analysis comparing the current product to our prototype.

After only three months on the job, I was ready to stop working underground and surface the proposal to the rest of the organization. I hoped my project would advance the UX maturity of the company and establish my credibility with my colleagues.

That's when I made the biggest political mistake of my career. Instead of collaborating with my peers in product management and development, I bypassed them and presented the project directly to the executive leadership team (ELT).

The ELT was enthusiastic and approved the project immediately. I thought I was home free. But then my colleagues in the Four-Legged Stool heard about the project through the company grapevine and were furious. The corporate immune system came at me full force.

They had a right to be resentful. Here I was, this new guy, getting all the credit for driving this great innovation for the company. Executives constantly called me out in meetings and praised the tremendous impact I was having, which only increased the tension.

It took time, but gradually I was able to repair my relationships with my partners in development and product management. As the project moved along, my colleagues contributed significant improvements to the original design. Had I engaged them earlier, we could have incorporated their suggestions before the sprints started and saved a lot of time and aggravation.

The new product, *MENTOR*, was a great success—a success attributable to the cross-functional team that gave birth to it. I may have conceived the project, but it required the efforts and expertise of people from every department in the company to see it through to completion.

Two words of advice:

Do work underground initially. Do the research, think it through, build a prototype, and compose a compelling story around it.

But...

Don't work underground for more than a month or so. Unless you enlist your product team to help shape your idea, you will engender enemies instead of allies.

That's how innovation gets done. That's how culture is changed. That's how users are served. That's how you fulfill your mission.

That's how you navigate the politics of UX.

INDEX

About John Scott Bowie

Forty years ago, I started my career as a technical writer at HP. Before long I was designing software user interfaces, and, through a lot of study and practice, transitioned into the nascent field of user experience design.

As my career progressed, I served as a UX engineer, scientist, project manager, teacher, and director, always as a UX insider with internal design teams in both multinational corporations and small privately held firms.

Today, I spend my time thinking about what's next for UX. I have so much more to learn. We will need new mindsets, new design frameworks, and new methodologies to move our profession forward.

Please stay in touch with me at john@coloradodesignlabs. I'm no longer "in the trenches" and I love hearing about your victories, your challenges, and the innovative ways you are raising our discipline to the next level.

Stay tuned for Volumes 2 and 3 of *Navigating the Politics of UX*, coming later in 2022.